Ascension:

The Art of Soul Perfection and the Attainment of Grace

Dr. Bruce Goldberg

Published by

Bruce Goldberg, Inc.
4300 Natoma Ave.
Woodland Hills, CA 91364
Telephone: (800) KARMA-4-U or
FAX: (818) 704-9189
Email: drbg@sbcglobal.net
Web Site:
www.drbrucegoldberg.com

Printed in the United States of America

ISBN 1-57968-019-4

Note to Reader:

This book is the result of the professional experiences accumulated by the author since 1974, working individually with over 14,000 patients. The material included here is intended to complement, not replace, the advice of your own physician, psychotherapist, or other health care professional, whom you should always consult about your circumstances prior to starting or stopping any medication or any other course of treatment, exercise regimen, or diet.

At times, the masculine pronoun has been used as a convention. It is intended to imply both male and female genders where this is applicable.

Some of the minor details in the case histories have been altered to protect the privacy of the author's patients. All of the names used, except those of the celebrities mentioned, have been altered. Everything else in these pages is true.

ABOUT THE AUTHOR

Dr. Bruce Goldberg holds a B.A. degree in Biology and Chemistry, is a Doctor of Dental Surgery, and has an M.S. degree in Counseling Psychology. He retired from dentistry in 1989, and has concentrated on his hypnotherapy practice in Los Angeles. Dr. Goldberg was trained by the American Society of Clinical Hypnosis in the techniques and clinical applications of hypnosis in 1975.

Dr. Goldberg has interviewed on *Coast to Coast AM, Oprah, Leeza, Joan Rivers, Regis, Tom Snyder, Jerry Springer, Jenny Jones,* and *Montel Williams* shows; by *CNN, NBC, Fox, CBS News,* and many others.

Through lectures, television and radio appearances, and newspaper articles, including interviews in *Time* The *Los Angeles Times, USA Today,* and the *Washington Post,* he has conducted more than 35,000 past-life regressions and future-life progressions since 1974, helping thousands of patients empower themselves through these techniques. His CDs, cassette tapes and DVDs teach people self-hypnosis, and guide them into past and future lives. He gives lectures and seminars on hypnosis, regression and progression therapy, and conscious dying; he is also a consultant to corporations, attorneys, and the local and network media. His first edition of *The Search for Grace,* was made into a television movie by CBS. His third book, the award winning *Soul Healing,* is a classic on alternative medicine and psychic empowerment. *Past Lives—Future Lives* is Dr. Goldberg's international bestseller and is the first book written on future lives (progression hypnotherapy).

Dr. Goldberg distributes CDs, cassette tapes, and DVDs to teach people self-hypnosis and to guide them into past and future lives and time travel. For information on self-hypnosis tapes, speaking engagements, or private sessions, Dr. Goldberg can be contacted directly by writing to:

Bruce Goldberg, D.D.S., M.S.
4300 Natoma Avenue, Woodland Hills, CA 91364
Telephone: (800) Karma-4-U or (800) 527-6248
Fax: (818) 704-9189
email: drbg@sbcglobal.net
Website: www.drbrucegoldberg.com

Please include a self-addressed, stamped envelope with your letter.

OTHER BOOKS BY
DR. BRUCE GOLDBERG

Past Live, Future Lives
Soul Healing
*The Search for Grace: A Documented Case of Murder
and Reincarnation*
*Peaceful Transition: The Art of Conscious Dying and the
Liberation of the Soul*
New Age Hypnosis
*Karmic Capitalism: A Spiritual Approach to Financial
Independence*
Unleash Your Psychic Powers
*Look Younger and Live Longer: Add 25 to 50 Quality
Years to Your Life Naturally*
*Protected by the Light: The Complete Book of Psychic
Self Defense*
*Time Travelers from Our Future: A Fifth Dimension
Odyssey*
*Astral Voyages: Mastering the art of Interdimensional
Travel*
Custom Design Your Own Destiny
*Self-Hypnosis: Easy Ways to Hypnotize Your Problems
Away*
*Dream Your Problems Away: Heal Yourself While You
Sleep*
*Egypt: An Extraterrestrial and Time Traveler
Experiment*
Past Lives, Future Lives Revealed

Contents

*B*ecoming aware of our soul as one with God is called different things by society. Some refer to it as transcendence, others as a form of an existential bliss. Christians might label this as the attainment of grace. I simply call it ascension.

Within each one of us resides a type of spiritual consciousness that assists us in our path back to God, from whence we came. This can be accomplished only when our karma is eliminated, and our soul reaches a state of perfection.

This book will present an approach that combines Eastern and Western paradigms and techniques to purify our soul. Although you may be familiar with the physical realm of the universe around us, there are other levels of which you may not be aware.

Throughout this book we will discuss and experience these other planes or dimensions. Each of the realms that make up our karmic cycle, including the physical world, is both transient and illusionary. It is your inner world of consciousness or soul that is true reality. Joy, peace and love dominate this inter universe, while sensations and various temptations steering us from our path of spiritual growth are emphasized in the physical realm.

As you become attuned to your soul, you will once again experience peace. When your emotions and thoughts are quieted, you can be prepared to receive that which is of God.

The very fact that you are reading this book suggests a wanting or thirst for both knowledge and experience of knowingness. When you cross that threshold into a spiritual knowingness you begin to make a commitment from your heart of hearts to change and grow toward God.

By moving your consciousness into the soul and experiencing the pure wonders of the universe, your ability to learn and forgive magnifies. This greatly facilitates your soul's ability to prepare itself for its final movement, ascension to God.

Certain signs will be noted by you as you enter this path of knowingness. Letting go of old experiences as they become complete, and losing the tendency to hang on to these old ways are the most common initial steps to the path leading to ascension.

You are much more than your body, your feeling and thoughts. As information is received by you from your Higher Self, a manifestation of love is felt all through your very being. Now you begin to live free and in the moment. No longer are you hung up on the past, or worried about the future.

All actions will be directed toward awakening your soul from its Earth plane sleep to a far more enlightened level of consciousness. Fears, prejudices and judgments slowly disappear from your awareness as you evolve spiritually.

This is again related to clearing out your past unresolved creations (karma), and conducting this cleansing under grace. Your mind will be trained throughout this book to maintain its consciousness and direct this process.

We will discuss and present exercises in meditation, yogic postures and breathing approaches and hypnosis to accomplish these goals. You will be professionally guided to draw your awareness to the exact point where God joins your very essence. The resulting expansion of this awareness will allow God to reveal the truth to you once and for all. It will be like no other you have read or thought of on your own.

Jesus said, "The kingdom of heaven is within." This kingdom can be reached by a combination of actions (loving and forgiving others, yourself and all things) and spiritual exercises that are presented throughout this book.

You will be shown via these exercises that it is not necessary to die to experience the other realms, including God. Another benefit attainable from this book is the solution to your eternal quest to finally eliminate karma. We will learn how to use our dream level to purify our soul.

Remember, the soul does not have to suffer to grow. Learning can be accomplished safely and peaceably through establishing a link with the perfect part of our soul, the Higher Self.

I do not present this work as a new religion. This paradigm need not conflict with any religious or spiritual belief you may currently follow. My patients come from various religious backgrounds. Whether they are Buddhist, Catholic, Jewish, Protestant, Moslem and so on does not negate their ability to use the philosophy and methods I present, while still retaining ties to their religious beliefs.

It has always been my belief that each of us is going

through the experiences we need in order to grow spiritually and to complete our karma. Ascension techniques will assist us in freeing ourselves once and for all from the cycle of birth and death. Eventually we will return to God.

*W*hen our soul reaches a level of sinlessness by the fulfillment of God's will, we refer to this as a state of grace. This condition has been described as a time of free unmerited love and favor of God. A reconciliation to God for further spiritual improvement and edification is also a component to attaining grace.

Once the state of grace is reached, only willful mortal sin can nullify this condition. In Christian practice habitual grace is first obtained through baptism of infants, or through either baptism or an act of perfect contrition in the case of adults.

Christian theology emphasizes that unless a soul is in the state of grace at the moment of death, it cannot attain the Beatific Vision. I refer to this vision as ascension to the God plane, and we will see how to attain this ascension as this book evolves.

There are many divergent opinions about attaining the state of grace in Christian circles. One point of agreement concerns St. Thomas Aquinas' view that one cannot have the position of grace until that person has experienced a special revelation from God.

St. Thomas emphasizes a "conjecture" or what we refer

to today as moral certitude of this natural truth. This is defined as a knowledge that excludes all prudent or positive doubt. We can reach this state only when we are free of sin. Signs of this pure state are fervor in prayer, delight in the things of God, the practice of mortification, avoiding sin, and so on.

God Himself represents uncreated grace. The decree to glorify those who will be saved by God is universally acknowledged by theologians. Every supernatural gift is grace, and God Himself is preeminent among these.

The Relationship Between Grace and Nature

There is a delicate balance between grace and nature. Grace is not due to nature, and yet it is divinely given to nature. The Church has always preached that human beings *must* attain grace if they are to attain eternal life.

Pelagius denied the concept of original sin and predestination. According to Pelagius (c. A.D.360-420), people have an inherent capacity for good. This stimulated St. Augustine to formulate his views on nature and grace. Augustine stated that a person's nature is wounded, hurt, damaged and destroyed by the willful disobedience of sin. He upheld the doctrines of original sin and divine grace.

Pelagius's teachings became known as Pelagianism, and this resulted in a series of synods with St. Augustine. Pelagius held firmly to his convictions that we have a freedom of choice to commit a sin or to resist that temptation. This would eventually give rise to the concept of free will. Eventually, Pope Innocent I condemned Pelagianism in A.D. 417 and excommunicated Pelagius.

We can look to St. Thomas for the notion that while grace

now is necessary to heal wounded nature, its primary function is to elevate nature to a share in the properly divine nature. Grace makes nature transcend itself, although it is rooted in nature throughout this process. Each of us has the capacity for this elevation.

During the Reformation, Augustine's indictment of man's sinful nature was strengthened. These new Protestants felt that free will itself was only capable of sin. The Catholic Church countered with its philosophy justifying grace and reaffirming the nature by which man's soul is elevated in Christ.

Here we see the difference in man's potential. The Protestants, through the works of Jansen, Baius and their disciples, limited grace as a mechanism that restores man, at best, to the primitive (natural) state just prior to original sin. They could not conceive of grace as something that allows man to transcend the order of nature.

Following World War II, a new theology was ushered in. This approach compromised the transcendent quality of the order of grace. These theologians felt an Extrinsicism was required and relegated grace to a mere superstructure added to nature.

The new theologians made openness to grace a constituent of man's nature, and reduced the concept of 'pure nature' to an unrealizable abstraction. Pope Pius XII referred to this new theology as a deadly fruit. He stated, "Others destroy the gratuity of the supernatural order, since God, they say, cannot create intellectual beings without ordering and calling them to the beatific vision."[1]

Catholic theology maintains three main positions on the relationship between grace and nature. These can be described as:

1. Grace elevates nature.
2. Grace heals nature.
3. The harmony of grace and nature.

Grace Elevates Nature

Nature is the fundamental principle of every activity and receptivity because it signifies the very essence of everything. It is a reality that is fixed, well determined and consists of stable laws.

It is a free act of God that creates nature. God created man as a finite intellectual being endowed with all the essential characteristics we commonly attribute to human nature. The blessing God has granted the world through Christ constitutes a true *divinization* of sinful man. Redemption is a positive sharing of the divine nature, as well as the remission of sin.

Through faith, hope and charity, man's divinization is revealed. The final glory of a face-to-face vision of God represents the apex of this mechanism. Man's native powers are incapable of attaining this state. It is only through a divine nature that man may be capable of entering into an immediate union of knowledge and love with the divine being.

---

[1] Pope Pius XII, "Humani generis" in Albert Dondrune's <u>Foi chretienne et oensee contemporaine: les problemes philosophiques souleves dans 1' encyclique Humani generis</u>, 2nd Edition. (Louvain: Publications universitaires de Louvain, 1952).

Consequently, to divinize man means to elevate him to a level of perfection transcending his own nature. Since it entirely transcends the powers and exigencies of man's nature, divinizing grace is something to which nature can lay no claim. Arising in the mystery of God's self-giving love, grace can only be received in grateful wonder at the eternal miracle of love that it is.

Grace Heals Nature

Man's nature is not beyond redemption because of original sin. This wounding is explained by the fact that as a consequence of original sin, mankind lost the supernatural gift of grace and the gratuitous preternatural gifts, but that its natural perfections are undiminished.

Another explanation is offered by the Thomist school, which states that the loss of original justice brings a profound lowering of nature's tendency to virtue. By restoring the elevation sin negated and by eliminating the obstacle that prevents nature toward establishing virtue, grace progressively heals the wounds of nature. Only when divinization is total will its healing restore the equivalent of the lost preternatural gifts.

The Harmony of Grace and Nature

God orders nature to grace and creation to redemption. Only man has an openness to grace, since we are created in the image of God.' No lower creature has this potential. It is through God's creation of the world and of man to Christ that humanity is given the opportunity to participate in the inner life of God.

We are all capable of beatific vision, since God created us as intellectual beings open to the Supreme Being. It is possible for man to be elevated to this undue, supernatural, face-to-face vision of God. Revelation assures us that this is a real possibility and meant to be fulfilled. St. Thomas never speaks of a natural desire for the beatific vision, but he does emphasize a natural desire to see God.

Other theologians propose that man does have an innate desire for perfect beatitude. We must remember that the perfect beatitude of the intellectual creature can be had only in the satisfaction of his unlimited capacity for being and goodness. Nothing short of beatific vision can satisfy this natural longing, and so these theologians conclude that there is in man's nature an innate natural desire for the beatific vision, though it can reach its goal only through the gracious intervention of God.

Still another view avers that by the free determination of God, man was actually created in grace and has never had any real destiny other than a supernatural one. The absence of grace is now more than a mere absence, it is a true privation.

An Example of Beatific Vision

St. Paul was preoccupied with the persecution of Christians until he received his beatific vision on the road to Damascus. This apostle encountered a great light and in an instant his life was changed. He became a leading proponent of Christianity, despite the ridicule he suffered when he tried to tell others of his experience. Was this not his karmic retribution?

Paul's conversion resulted in his temporary blindness on the physical plane, but a far more visionary advancement on other levels. He now viewed things differently and understood far better the mysteries of our existence. These he tried to explain to others but found it difficult to convey such new and strange ideas to minds that were not yet ready. He preached sermons, he gave classes and he wrote letters to his students and followers. Those letters that have been preserved are known as the Epistles of St. Paul.

Writings preserving Paul's preaching to his students at Corinth describes the psychic development characteristic of this form of spiritual awakening. He referred to psychic energy as the gift of the Spirit. He states:

7. But the manifestation of the Spirit is given to every man to profit withal.
8. For to one is given the Spirit of the word of wisdom; to another the word of knowledge by the same Spirit.
9. To another faith by the same Spirit; to another the gifts of healing by the same Spirit;
10. To another the working of miracles; to another prophecy; to another discerning of spirits; to another interpretation of tongues.
11. But all these worketh that one and the selfsame Spirit; dividing to every man severally as he will.[2]

These gradual steps to attaining grace are facilitated by our psychic development. We must access our Higher Self to manifest these gifts. When we accomplish this, our road to ascension is all the more facilitated. Our free will determines

---

[2] I Cor. 12:7-11.

how and to what extent these gifts of the Spirit are acquired and utilized.

Usually this process of illumination is quite gradual. Sometimes one first sees little flashes of light, called 'stars,' when a truth is spoken or when a new idea strikes. These are gone in an instant, a fraction of a second. Later, usually when at ease with the eyes closed, a broader flash of brilliant light will appear, light very much like the brightest sunlight. This too lasts but an instant, but when it is repeated it lingers a little longer each time. Slowly our inner vision is developed and grace or ascension is then attainable.

The Eastern Mechanism of Grace

Although we associate the term grace with Western Christian theology, the Easterners have their own equivalent. The Egyptians professed the concept of the *Ka*, which corresponds to the metaphysical astral body. The Ka is really the vehicle of the soul, not the soul itself. This is equivalent to the astral body being the vehicle of the mind and soul today.

The Ka visited the mummified body from time to time. A birdlike double represented this Ka in Egyptian paintings. In order for the soul of the dead person to attain the Christian equivalent of grace, it had to wander through the Under World and pass many tests. This is described in detail in the Egyptian *Book of the Dead.*[3]

The ancient Egyptians believed that their god Osiris could give eternal life to the souls who approached him following death. Osiris's body was resurrected following his earthly

---

[3] E. A. Wallis Budge, "The Book of the Dead" (London: Longman's & Co., 1895).

sojourn, and he was solely responsible for the granting of grace to those who requested it.

In the famous Judgment Scene of *The Book of the Dead* contained in the Papyrus of Ani, the scribe Ani's heart is weighed on a scale or balance against a feather, representing truth and right. These ancients did not believe in either a general resurrection or a prolonged purgatory. A human-headed hawk standing on a pylon represents Ani's soul. The deceased addresses his heart and prays that he will be granted eternal life(ascension).

After the heart is weighed, Ani declares that he is righteous and holy (in a state of grace) and has not sinned against the gods. If he has, the monster Amemet or the Eater of the Dead' will descend upon him. Upon a successful weighing of his heart, the soul is granted freedom to pass into the regions of the dominion of Osiris and enter into everlasting life and happiness. This is the essence of ascension.

The Tibetan Book of the Dead

The *Bardo Thödol*, or Tibetan *Book of the Dead*,[4] gives us the Tibetan mechanism for attaining grace and eventual ascension of the soul. This sacred scripture was first written down during the eighth century A.D., and compiles teachings that are far more ancient.

This scripture encompasses the same general topic as is depicted in the Egyptian *Book of the Dead*, but the *Bardo Thöbol* is far easier to relate to the Western mind. The teachings presented in *The Tibetan Book of the Dead*

---

[4] W. Y. Evans-Wenz, "The Tibetan Book of the Dead" (New York: Oxford University Press, 1960).

correspond with those of the occult sciences and metaphysics.

When a person is about to die, a lama is summoned to guide the soul properly into the next world. This guide presses the arteries on the sides of the neck to keep the dying person conscious, with the consciousness rightly directed. The nature of the death-consciousness determines the future state of the soul-complex, existence being the continuous transformation of one conscious state to another. The pressing of the arteries regulates the path to be taken by the outgoing vital current (Prana).

The lama continuously urges the dying individual to keep this mind tranquil and poised, so that he may see and enter into the Clear Light of Reality, and may not be troubled with hallucinations or thought-forms that have no objective existence, except within the individual's own mind. If everything goes according to plan, this process takes about three and one- half to four days. The presence of the priest can shorten this process. Separation of the astral body from the physical at death is known as the extractor-of-the-consciousness principle. The lama or priest who supervises this mechanism is called hypho-bo (pronounced pho-o).

If the deceased has not been properly concentrated upon the Clear Light, he is liable to see scores of devils and demons of all kinds. These entities have no actual objective existence, they are merely thought-forms created by the consciousness of the departed. These symbolic beings must be properly dealt with, as the departed soul moves on to the Clear Light of the Void. The sooner he can do this, the sooner is his or her attainment of grace or ascension achieved. The *Bardo Thödol* describes the journey of the astral body as follows:

"When thou were recovered from the swoon (of death) thy Knower must have risen up in its primordial condition and a radiant body, resembling the former body, must have sprung forth. . . . It is called the desire-body. . . . The Bardo-body hath been spoken of as 'endowed with all sense-faculties.' . . . Unimpeded motion implyeth that thy present body being only a desire body is not a body of gross matter. . . . Thou art actually endowed with the power of miraculous motion. . . . Ceaselessly and involuntarily wilt thou be wandering about. To all those who are weeping (thou shalt say) 'Here I am, weep not.' But they not hearing thee, thou wilt think, 'I am dead!' And again, at that time, thou wilt be feeling very miserable. Be not miserable in that way. . . . There will be a grey, twilight-like light, both by night and by day, and at all times. . . . Even though thou seekest a body, thou wilt gain nothing but trouble. Put aside the desire for a body; and permit they mind to abide in the state of resignation, and act so as to abide therein. . . ."[5]

There are six different bardo, or in-between-life, states described in the Mahayana Buddhist tradition. These are known as:

1. Bardo of Birth
2. Lifetime Bardo
3. Bardo of the Moments before Death
4. Bardo of the Moments after Death
5. Deathtime Bardo
6. Bardo of the Moment before Birth

---

[5] W. Y. Evans-Wentz, op. cit.

The *Tibetan Book of the Dead* is divided into three parts. The *Chikhai Bardo* relates the psychic details of the moment of death. The second component is known as the *Chonyid Bardo,* and concerns itself with the karmic illusions immediately following death. The *Sidpa Bardo* is the last part and deals with the onset of rebirth.

Enlightenment, or liberation, is possible for the sojourning soul at any time during the 49-day bardo cycle. If the soul passes a series of tests, it is liberated and may ascend to join Buddha (god). This is the Tibetan equivalent of attaining a state of grace.

Each of the bardo states are separated by a swoon, or temporary loss of consciousness. The voyaging soul is constantly reminded to merge with the Clear Light (the Higher Self). This merging will immediately result in the liberation of the soul from the karmic cycle of birth and death.

The soul will meet various peaceful and wrathful Buddhas as part of their tests. The wrathful Buddha is the dark side of one of the Peaceful Buddhas. The Wrathful Buddhas appear in the same order as their Peaceful counterparts. The person is instructed to recognize these, too, as aspects of their consciousness, and to unite with them. In merging with a Wrathful Buddha, the person will obtain Buddahood (grace) and spend his or her remaining, between-life time in the peaceful, divine realm of mind associated with the Peaceful counterpart of the Wrathful Buddha. In running away, the person will only fall into deeper and more terrifying levels of the intermediate state.

On the thirteenth and fourteenth days, the persons who have not recognized the darker sides of themselves represented by the Wrathful Buddhas perceive 58 other Wrathful deities (including eight Gaurima, eight Takenma, four doorkeepers and twenty-eight Wang Chuk Ma). If these are not recognized, then all of the Wrathful deities appear jointly as the Lord of Death. The Lord of Death dismembers the person who, despite great pain, cannot die. This symbolizes the difficulty of extinguishing the lesser, ego-self as the person clings to this self-image.

One of the lessons presented by the Bardo Thödol is to face death calmly and heroically and with a clear mind. The hypho-bo is a necessary component to the Tibetan's system of what I call conscious dying, for three reasons:

(1) The initiates need to be reminded of their spiritual preparation for death, especially if they lack alertness during this critical time; (2) the dying need to be surrounded with helpful thoughts during the initial stages of bardo without allowing emotional attachments to depress their spirit; and (3) the voyager should treat every moment of his or her life as if it were the last.

The state of grace is finally achieved when the voyager establishes dominion over the realm of death, and, being able to perceive death's illusory nature, is freed from fear. A cleansing of all sins is automatically accomplished at this exact moment, thus allowing for ascension. My main thesis in this discussion is to illustrate the fact that our soul must be perfect and in a state of grace in order to ascend to the God plane to join the Creator of the universe.

The Path to the State of Grace

In order to place yourself on the path to attain the state of grace, there are certain things you need to do and to avoid. First, you need to give up seeking God in the manner to which you have been accustomed.

This may sound like a radical statement, and one in which I may be advocating dissolving ties with all formal religions, or just plain heresy. In actuality, it is none of these. I am not advocating a change in your creed (belief), merely an alteration in the manner in which you act.

If your current system of behavior were perfect, or well within the path to grace, you wouldn't be reading this book. Your status now would consist of ascension to God. The frustration experienced by scattered attention and diametrically opposed belief systems and actions has resulted in a stunting of your spiritual growth.

Think about your life for a moment. Do you not have myriad unresolved problems and face stress every day? This is not conducive to being on the path to the attainment of grace.

We must cut through the maze and place ourselves (no one can do this for you) on the path to grace. The spark of divine consciousness is within all of us. All we have to do is recognize it and work with it. It is by trusting in our heart of hearts with pure motives that we can attain the transcendent state known as grace. Accompanying this process will be a change in our concepts of reality.

It is critical to establish an agreement with God to have His audience. Jesus spoke of this principle in his Sermon on the Mount. Buddha discussed this concept in his Eight Noble Truths. To attain this state of grace we must be able to allow our spirit to control and calm the mind.

The five passions of anger, vanity, lust, greed and undue

attachment to material things must be supplanted with a spiritual focus. We will utilize various methods to accomplish this goal. Through altered states of consciousness (ASCs), a quieting of the mind and control over our emotions will be initiated.

Some of these techniques will involve actual out-of-body experiences (OBEs). This is a simulation of what you will eventually experience when ascension is finally complete. The best ways to establish an agreement with God are to be in accord with right living and by becoming a divine channel for His love.

Once we reach this state of grace all things in our lives will be attended to. Our establishment of freedom, wisdom, love and other noble principles will ensure our eternal bliss. Each of us has a component of the God consciousness within our spirit or soul. We refer to this perfect energy as the Higher Self or superconscious mind.

This Higher Self is our perfect immortal soul that establishes contact with God and freely operates without the restrictions contained in the material world. It is neither necessary nor desirable to seek God actively. We are always in the presence of the God energy, so we are only distracting ourselves by this artificial pursuit.

The process of attaining grace involves facilitating the expression of our Higher Self through our soul. We are created in the image of God because the state of grace is our natural destiny. This process consists of our functioning as a channel for God through our Higher Self as a type of agent.

One of our purposes spiritually is to allow the grace of God the opportunity to use each one of us as a vehicle for this supreme consciousness. The reward for this is ascension and liberation of our soul from the wheel of birth and death, known as karma.

Through the practice of the exercises I present in this book, we will begin the path to self-realization, and well on our way to God-realization. The various Masters and Saints have known these principles throughout history. By expanding our consciousness through ASCs our questions will be answered, and our soul purified. We all have this God-given talent to transcend the material world and attain these realizations.

We can look to discipline of our mind to make our journey toward grace easier. We are free when our mind is strong and the heart pure with love. The moment we truly identify with God we are in the sought-after state of grace.

The late Gina Cerminara studied the readings of America's greatest psychic Edgar Cayce. She set forth her understanding of Cayce's philosophy as follows:

- God exists.
- Every soul is a portion of God. (You are a soul; you inhabit a body.)
- Life is purposeful.
- Life is continuous.
- All human life operates under law.
  (Karma; reincarnation.)
- Love fulfills that law.
- The will of man creates his destiny.
- The mind of man has formative power.
- The answer to all problems is within the Self.

In the assurance of the above postulates, man is enjoined as follows:

- Realize first your relationship to the Creative Forces of the Universe, or God.
- Formulate your ideals and purposes in life.
- Strive to achieve those ideals.
- Be active.
- Be patient.
- Be joyous.
- Leave the results to God.
- Do not seek to evade any problem.
- Be a channel of good to other persons.[6]

By understanding these principles and following a rightly directed lifestyle, we are all assured of attaining the state of grace. I had the pleasure of interviewing Gina on my radio show titled *Insights into Parapsychology* in 1982.

She impressed me as a quality soul, and I trust this quality individual practiced these principles and attained her state of grace. Gina left the Earth plane several years ago, but her work is well represented. She touched everyone who had exposure to her energy.

---

[6] Gina Cerminara, "Many Mansions" (New York: Signet, 1967), p. 226.

*W*hen we discuss the concept of truth a certain amount of subjectivity is involved. Our own individual consciousness determines what we feel is the truth. The absolute or ultimate truth cannot be deduced by way of our five senses, but only through consciousness and accessing our Higher Self.

The true form of spiritual truth is distorted by the physical senses. By separating our soul from the emotional and physical nature of our being, we are able to realize truth directly.[1] Keeping ourselves on the spiritual path toward grace and maintaining a constant connection with our Higher Self make this goal much easier to attain. Lack of knowledge and poor discipline function as distractors that detour us from our spiritual path.

The truth cannot be realized through philosophy, religion, willpower or mysticism alone. It is only when we allow the perfect energy of God to manifest in us that we are placed in a position to receive our truth. Each of us will formulate a different truth based on our own experiences, level of spiritual development and exposure to higher levels of awareness.

---

[1] B. Goldberg, "Peaceful Transition: The Art of Conscious Dying and the Liberation of the Soul" (St. Paul: Llewellyn, 1997).

Enlightenment is the term we apply when we receive this truth. A broader and deeper view of all things well beyond our five senses is developed within our consciousness. Much of this occurs in between lifetimes, but the techniques presented in this book will foster this spiritual evolvement in our physical plane sojourn.

Fear is always at the top of the list of factors that impede spiritual growth. Almost everyone fears death, and this tendency increases as we age. Many elderly patients of mine initially describe their fear of death as entering a dark world, where there is nothing but a black void.

Regardless of their theological orientation, they do not consider the possibility of a great adventure awaiting—a journey to other dimensions or planes, and an overview of the universal worlds. Even if they believe in reincarnation and God, the personal application of this paradigm, as their time on the physical plane draws to a close, is most often associated with anxiety and trepidation.

I will discuss the different dimensions in detail in Chapter 5. For our current purpose, let me reemphasize the importance of the exercises presented in this book to acquaint you with what you will experience when you cross into spirit, or clinically die.

Eventually, we all will end our current physical sojourn. Then the truth of what lies beyond, as well as our own personal truth, will be made available to us. There is absolutely no advantage of suffering from torment, pain or fear of death.

Ascension removes you from the cycle of birth and death, and allows you to enter the heavenly worlds to join God. You do have the option of remaining on these lower planes as a guide, but free of the discomforts you currently experience.

It must always be remembered that we exist as a microcosm in a vast macrocosm of the universe. Only by allowing a greater consciousness to penetrate our very being can we grow spiritually and rise above the illusions of the physical plane that hide the truth from us.

The truth will show us that good and evil, beauty and ugliness as we have defined them do not exist. The higher planes do not incorporate the duality and limitations that we accept in our daily lives. Realization of the God level corresponds with a sense of all-comprehending indivisible things and all-transcending paradigms. This pure knowledge results in the purest and most concentrated form of ecstasy that man is capable of experiencing.

The divine consciousness in everything is felt and observed on these higher worlds. By seeking the truth now through very simple techniques, we can get a glimpse of this hidden unity of the God force in everything.

These truths are far beyond our intellectual grasp alone. We must have pure motives, eliminate the physical plane tendency for personal gain, experience love at its most basic and beautiful level, and follow the principles of right living.

In the beginning, these truths may appear to contradict themselves. This paradox will cease to exist as our own level of awareness and spiritual growth expands. The truths of the lower realms do not apply on the higher realms. Each dimension has its own truth which applies to it alone. These truths are always superseded by the truths of realms beyond it. Truth as we perceive it during our spiritual evolution is always relative to the ultimate truth.

To experience the truth we are seeking does not require a renunciation of our physical life as we have established it. It is only an alteration of the mind's programming and the fears and inhibitions that are consequences of society's brain-washing.

Our consciousness appears to take four different forms. The first type is the complete state of unconsciousness we experience throughout most of our sleep cycle. As I described in my book *Soul Healing*,[2] this theta and delta brain wave state of our brain is necessary for survival.

The REM cycle, or dream state, represents the second form of consciousness. Although our recall of dream images is often disorderly and disjointed, it is a natural out-of-body experience (OBE) that registers as an alpha wave on the electroencephalograph (EEG). This is the state of mind in which we have access to our Higher Self and greatly facilitate our spiritual growth.

The third example of consciousness is our waking state. We are most familiar with this state of mind characterized by receiving input from our five senses. The disadvantage of this state of consciousness is that we are at the mercy of our intellect and thereby most susceptible to the illusory physical plane. The truth we seek is easily hidden from us.

Finally, the fourth and most important type of consciousness we possess is our Higher Self or superconscious mind. This perfect component of our soul's energy is what we will eventually merge with when we are eligible for ascension.

---

[2] B. Goldberg, "Soul Healing" (St. Paul: Llewellyn, 1996).

Finding Your Ultimate Truth

The true test and mission of a soul is to find ultimate truth or reality. Unfortunately, religions present a rather one-sided view of this goal. None of these institutions are truly free of negative forces.

For example, can the Christians be right when they say that only those who believe in Jesus will attain grace? That would mean approximately 75 percent of the Earth's population is doomed to eternal damnation! The Buddhists, Islamists, Jews and others have their own paradigms.

These hard-nosed dogmas may sound impressive to the uninitiated and very impressionable souls who are regularly exposed to this propaganda, but someone is most definitely wrong. These divergent views aren't really healthy, they just function to polarize people and foster prejudice. Do we need any more religious wars?

When a prophet, social, moral or political reformer comes onto the public scene, many are taken in because they want to believe. Our laziness toward seeking our own ultimate truth is at play here.

These moral spokespeople may truly mean well. However, it is up to us as individuals to find our own truth and perfect our own soul. We must somehow concern ourselves with the totality of God. Our own efforts are required to transcend the morality and other limitations of the physical plane and become one with God.

The spiritual exercises presented in this book will assist you in finding your ultimate truth and eventual ascension. Practice them diligently and you will never doubt your eternal salvation.

Experience has taught me that there are four different types of seekers of truth. The first type take an intellectual approach. They read and discuss the theoretical paradigms, but never practice the recommended techniques. Their attitude is one of expecting everything to be done for them, and they demand instant results.

The second group comprises those who make an honest attempt at spiritual growth, but because they achieve less than desired goals, seek other avenues. The third type of truth seekers follow the spiritual exercises and most of the other suggestions, but cannot totally commit to this approach and reach only limited levels of advancement.

Finally, we have the students who follow the recommendations and commit themselves to a spiritual path. These successful graduates perfect their souls, attain eternal bliss and ascend to the God plane.

To find your ultimate truth you must be adventurous and bold. Be prepared to face many distractions and obstacles along your path to spiritual perfection. The world of illusions, and your defense mechanisms that dysfunctionally respond to them, are your greatest enemies in this quest.

My main point here is to encourage you not to place all your hopes on receiving salvation and redemption after your physical death, but to continually seek your ultimate truth while you still have a physical body. Our philosophies, religions and other creeds do not preach salvation here on Earth, and encourage co-dependency behaviors to attain this state after death. We alone are both capable of and responsible for attaining this soul liberation in this lifetime.

The Law of Karma

When I describe karmic laws my purpose is to present a paradigm, not *the* paradigm. You are certainly entitled to accept or reject any aspect of this Eastern philosophy. All I ask of you is to consider the logic of its basis and apply whatever component of it that suits your own spiritual path.

We must consider the law of cause and effect when discussing karma. This principle assists our understanding of our actions in that every action we undertake creates an equal and opposite reaction.

Karma helps the soul in its spiritual evolution by teaching the power of love and forgiveness. Its purpose is *not* to punish us. We punish ourselves. For example, if we deprived another human being of freedom in a previous life, we'd probably have our freedom curtailed in this life. This experience would give us time to reconsider our views and learn the law of love.

Understanding and accepting the law of karma in our lives eliminates the tendency to consider ourselves as a victim. Problems are now reclassified as opportunities for spiritual growth as we begin to see the spiritual big picture.

Karma encourages us to take charge of our lives. This new form of spiritual empowerment requires us to follow the highest code of ethics. This new behavior allows us to achieve an exalted state of self-realization in which we alone are held accountable for our actions.

One side effect of practicing the exercises I present is to eliminate the habits and attitudes that have bound you to the past and prevented you from finding your ultimate truth. A spiritual liberation from the cycle of birth and death, or wheel of karma, results.

If we view our life on Earth as only a single existence, God seems random, arbitrary and cruel. When we view an entire series of lifetimes or subcycle, it becomes clear that we are born again and again until we learn our spiritual lessons.

What we reap in this lifetime is truly what we have sown in another life. The laws of love and forgiveness must be mastered. Hurting or lashing back at another human being creates a karmic debt. This obligation will have to be paid. It is not God punishing us, but ourselves.

Our suffering is not always punishment for past actions. There are many subtle processes at work. If you experience fear and persecution in a past life, you may still carry these feelings in your psychic memory. You may experience unwarranted fear and anxiety in your current life. These fears may persist until we cleanse our soul through accessing our Higher Self and rise above this negativity.

Karma does end. We will no longer experience a certain negativity once the lesson is learned. The karmic debt is wiped out eternally. This moving on to the next lesson is spiritual growth.

Ascension cannot be bought or granted by anyone else. Our sins of the past cannot be absolved at the last minute simply by request. We earn spiritual wisdom by taking responsibility for our actions and by learning how to purify our own soul through communicating with our Higher Self and establishing a God-consciousness.

When we realize we are the creator of our own life a form of spiritual maturity is evident. By learning to be a co-worker with God we can create a reality that is the most beneficial for us all.

Preparing the Mind and Body For Seeking the Truth

A certain amount of discipline is required to attain any worthwhile goal. Spiritual growth and perfection is no exception. Going beyond our self-centered thoughts and committing our energy to assisting others and receiving the God consciousness is what I am referring to.

This is not a mindless submissiveness, nor a blind faith following of some doctrine. Love, care and responsibility are most definitely involved with this system. You will find your efforts will produce a rich and blissful experience if it is based upon clear and correct understanding of this sound principle.

Buddhism discusses the concept of refuge as the first step in soul awakening to the ultimate truth. Refuge is the attitude of relying upon, or turning to, something for guidance and help. We take refuge in friends for love and security, in food and entertainment when we are hungry and bored, for example.

These external forms of refuge are unreliable and represent codependencies at best. To the Buddhist refuge involves discovering and utilizing the unlimited potential that lies within each of us. There are two aspects of refuge, outer and inner. Outer refuge is appreciating upon the three jewels: buddha, dharma, and sangha. Buddha refers both to the enlightened state itself—the removal of all negative qualities and the perfection of all positive—and to those who have attained enlightenment. When we open our heart to the love and wisdom offered by loving beings and accepting their guidance on the spiritual path, we have engaged in this concept of refuge.

When we speak of the realizations that make up the various sequential steps to enlightenment, we are referring to dharma. This Sanskrit term literally means 'to hold.' Since Buddha's teachings come from his actual experience of eliminating every trace of confusion and negative energy from his mind, this refuge protects us from problems. We are exhibiting dharma when we practice a discipline that acts to awaken within ourselves the wisdom that every enlightened being has within its consciousness.

The spiritual community providing both support and inspiration to us represents sangha, which provides the help we need to make the practice actually work. Buddhic teaching recommends discussing problems and seeking solutions with a group of like-minded souls. By respecting the aid presented from these spiritual colleagues and accepting their assistance, we are illustrating the principle of refuge in sangha.

Our inner refuge is refuge representing our ultimate potential to find the truth. The three outer refuges have an inner equivalent. The seed of enlightenment that lies within our consciousness is our inner buddha. Our natural wisdom that can distinguish real from false represents our inner dharma. Finally, the guidance and inspiration that we impart to others constitute our inner sangha. We each have the potential to develop unlimited love, compassion and wisdom and to free ourselves from all negative energy. It is within our potential to reach the same level as Buddha and discover our ultimate truth.

Most of us take refuge in material things to deal with our insecurities, boredom, short attention span and low self-image in general. Contemplate for a moment what your life would be like if just for a day you removed yourself from all contact with television, newspapers, radio, magazines, computers, games and people.

Throughout this book I will present both theory and exercises to train you to be fulfilled and directed toward your spiritual path of truth by relying on your inner refuge.

Buddha's Four Holy Truths

My discussion of Buddhic doctrine is not meant to convert any of my readers to this philosophy. I present this ancient discipline to illustrate a path and a mechanism you can apply to find your path toward truth.

Buddha described what he called Four Holy Truths. The affirmation that all moral existence is characterized by dukkha is the first truth. Dukkha is a term that applies to what we would call evil, ill, disease and imperfect. When things in our lives are not what ideally they should be, or as we would like them to be, dukkha is manifested.

Samodaya is the sense of uneasiness that arises out of desire or craving, and represents the second truth. When we attempt to use ideas, experiences, things or other people to cater to our pleasures, we are illustrating this second truth.

The third Buddhic truth is a cessation of desire called nirodha. This elimination of desire is accompanied by the cessation of the experience of dukkha and represents nirvana. Nirvana is the attainment of the ideal state of being or ascension.

As a baby boomer, I grew up using the expression "cool". Little did I know that this term referred to Buddha's third truth. Nibbota is an Indian term that literally means 'cool.' This connotation actually refers to being cool after a fever, or healthy. Nibbota represents the ideal of being. It is a level of being 'cooled' from the heat of the passions of greed, hatred and illusion.

Fortunately, there is a mechanism to reach nirvana and eliminate such distracting desires. This pure state of being is reached by the magga, or path, developed by Buddha, and represents the fourth truth. As I stated earlier, we all have the potential to reach this state.

The Buddhic Path to the Truth

Buddha preached a three-fold path to enlightenment consisting of morality, meditation and wisdom. One is supposed to pursue these disciplines simultaneously. However, morality concepts must be immediately established to ensure the success of this approach.

There are five basic moral observances that are supposed to be incorporated into our daily lives and can be listed as follows:

- Refrain from causing injury to living things
- Do not steal
- Refrain from sexual immorality
- Do not tell lies
- Eliminate the use of alcohol and other drugs

Three additional observances were added by more advanced practitioners of Buddhism and are described as:

- Abstain from eating after midday
- Abstain from dancing, singing and amusements.
- Abstain from the use of garlands, cosmetics and personal adornments.

When Buddhists speak of 'taking the eight precepts' at a monastery on holy days, they are alluding to these eight moral observances. These observances are not to be confused with the Eightfold Path.

In order to acquire the ultimate truth, the Buddhists emphasize that a good moral life is a necessary foundation from which understanding of the true nature of things will be manifested. As part of your spiritual growth, try following these eight precepts for a period of 24 hours. They can be taken any time, but the days of the new, full and quarter moons are recommended. I recommend a period of sunrise to sunrise for initiation into this discipline.

There are many advantages of incorporating these precepts into your lifestyle. Among these are:

- The development of a clear and uncluttered mind
- Greater ease at meditation and self-hypnosis
- The ability to avoid negative future lives
- Attracting higher quality spiritual guides in your current and future lives
- Reaching the state of ascension and avoiding the need to reincarnate.

Meditation

Meditation is the second component of Buddhic discipline. In Chapter 8, I will present several exercises and the mechanics of this ancient discipline in greater detail. For our current discussion, consider the promise that right thought and right attitude are correlated with right being.

One of the primary goals of meditation is the cultivation

of right thought and right (morally wholesome) attitudes. The Buddhic Eightfold Path describes the interrelation of thought and action. We may consider these eight items as follows:

- Right understanding of the nature of the world and the human situation
- Right thought, or a right inner mental attitude
- Right speech
- Right bodily action
- Right livelihood
- Right moral effort
- Right mindfulness
- Right concentration

These eight paths are preceded by a development of faith in the ability to ultimately receive the truth and attain nirvana. What is initially accepted in faith becomes a matter of wisdom or direct knowledge. It is now possible to reach your ultimate truth.

Wisdom

Buddha's truth regarding wisdom incorporates several elements. We have already discussed the fact that all mortal life is dukkha. Annica means impermanence, and is another component of our physical life. Nothing in our world remains unchanged. The universe is in a continual state of flux.

A third aspect of Buddhic wisdom is that of Anatta. This truth states that there is no permanent or unchanging soul (atman) contained within our body. We each consist of a temporary conjunction of five groups of factors known as khandhas. One of these groups is physical, and the remaining four nonphysical.

These five groups can be listed as follows:

- Physical form
- Sensation
- Perception
- Volition
- Consciousness

Buddha declared that these five groups are in constant flux and cease to exist when physical death occurs. This is rather controversial in that Buddha believed that nothing associated with the isolated human individual is eternal.

This denial of reality of the individual soul distinguished Buddhism from all other religions in India. The heretical nature of this paradigm revolved around the concept that if there is no permanent soul, why should we care how we live? Without an eternal soul to reincarnate in a future life, one would not bear the consequences of their good or evil actions.

An unorthodox Buddhic sect arose known as the Personalists, who stated that although Buddha denied the reality of the soul, he must have affirmed the reality of the person as the enduring basis of being. We must always bear in mind Buddha's concept of the illusionary aspect of the physical plane. The individual soul, he felt, was merely a component of this illusion.

By advocating moral and meditative disciplines, Buddha suggested that these means would function to eliminate the illusory nature of our world by our perception. He was affirming the reality of a wider realm of being, not limited by the 'I,' 'me,' 'mine' mentality of society.

To ascend we must overcome the natural tendency to crave and desire Earthly things. We must reach a desire-free life to experience nirvana. No other short-cut or diversion can facilitate this state of pure being.

The Law of Karma

According to the law of karma every deliberate action results in an equal consequence or reaction that can persist into future incarnations. According to the Jainist sect of India, molecules that constitute our organs of speech, mind and body when activated produce vibrating (yoga) in the soul and attract karmic matter that pervades space.

The soul is not bound by this mechanism unless actuated by passions (kashaya) such as attachment or aversion, and participates in evil actions. When this happens the karmic matter is absorbed by the soul.

In seeking your truth consider this concept of karma. The Jainists classify seven types of karma as follows:

- Knowledge – obscuring karma is brought on by envy and produces low intelligence
- Feeling – producing karma results from self-pity and unpleasant feelings are its sequella.
- Faith – deluding karma brings on disbelief in the true nature of reality.
- Conduct – deluding karma is due to intense feelings and passions and can result in a lack of restraint from evil acts.

- Life – determining karma is responsible for the span of our life
- Status – determining karma dictates how high or low our status is within each lifetime
- Obstructive karma prevents our achieving desired goals, especially those involved with giving and gaining enjoyment.

The only way to end this cycle of birth and death and karmic carryover is by arresting the passions and by redirecting the channels of their activity. This can be accomplished by the Buddha's Eightfold Path. Ascension is the ultimate state of being, as it constitutes the path to liberation.

The Hermetic Writings

In seeking the truth we should not overlook the writings reportedly authored by an ancient Egyptian priest known as Hermes Trismegistus (thrice-greatest). This transmitter of ancient Egyptian wisdom was thought to have lived not long after the time of Moses.

The antiquity of Hermes is confirmed by St. Augustine. The writings of Hermes have survived in a treatise known as the Asclepius and the collection of treatises are grouped together as the Corpus Hermeticum.[3] Some additional fragments are preserved in the Stubaeus anthologies.

Heremes Trismegistus is supposedly the Egyptian god Thoth. These writings are in the form of dialogues and relate to discussions held between Tat (Thoth), Ammon, Horus, Isis

---

[3] Hermes Trismegistus, "Corpus Hermeticum." Trans. A. J. Festugiere and A.D. Nock (Paris: Societe Edition Les Pelles Lettres, 1945-1954).

and the healing gods Imhotep and Asclepius.

The main purpose behind these dialogues is to teach the understanding of man, God and the universe, and instruct man on the art of ascension. Hermetism has been compared to gnosticism, since the latter also teaches that the human soul can escape from its bondage to matter only if it possesses the true knowledge or understanding (the gnosis), which is the privilege of a select few.

In the first text of the Corpus Hermeticum, Hermes describes his communication with a superhuman being, Poimandres, the spirit of omnipotence. At death, Poimandres explains, man abandons the body, the senses and the two lower parts of the soul: passion and desire. Then he ascends through the spheres of the seven planets, leaving behind him in each of them part of his being, the part which the original man had received from the stars. Finally he will be reduced to just himself and can enter the eighth sphere and join the powers assembled there. With them he comes before the Father and enters God.

In the Asclepius text Hermes informs us that man must show piety toward God and, by order of God and together with Him, to rule the Earthly world. The main virtues of men are piety and a contempt for the body and matter. Whoever cooperates with God merits release from his mission in the world and a return to the godlike life of the pure spirit. Those who fail to do this are reborn after death in other forms.

The Hermetic writings discuss the concept of judgment. Physical death is followed by a judging of the soul and either a reward of eternal bliss or a punishment of offenders. Repeated themes of the fact that spirit is good and matter and the body are evil are present throughout this ancient work.

Man must live in conformity with the spirit, which means that he must try to know God and to share with God the task of administering the world of matter. Understanding and piety are the only important things. The Hermetic authors stress only one virtue, that of piety in longing to know and understand God, the world and man.

Sidney Spencer's book, *Mysticism in World Religion*, thoroughly presents Hermetic doctrines. He states:

"For the Hermetists . . . it is through mystical experience that man attains liberation. In that experience, at its greatest intensity, the soul is wholly absorbed in the vision of God. 'Father,' says Tat to Hermes, 'you have given me my fill of this good and most beautiful sight, and my mind's eye is almost blinded by the splendour of the vision.'"

In another tractate the writer suggests that it is possible to rise to the knowledge of God, which implies identification with Him, by the application of the principle that 'like is apprehended by like.'

'Expand thyself into the immeasurable greatness passing beyond all bodily limits; raise thyself above all time, become eternal. Then thou shalt know God.' A man is to transcend all spatial and temporal limits – to 'become higher than all height, lower than all depth,' to take to himself 'the qualities of all creatures,' to conceive himself to be in every place, in the living and the dead. By such an expansion of the range of his consciousness man may rise into oneness with God, who is Himself the Whole."[4]

---

[4] Sidney Spencer, "Mysticism in World Religion" (New York: Penguin, 1963).

We can most certainly learn quite a bit about seeking the truth and ascension from the Hermetic writings. What we refer to as New Age paradigms was termed metaphysics by Aristotle and greatly expounded by Plato before him. New Age concepts go back much farther, possibly to the time of Moses.

The ancients knew about ascension principles and how to obtain the truth. As we progress in this book you will be presented with additional concepts to assist you in your own quest to acquire your truth.

Chapter 3:
Building A Bridge from
East to West

_____

A discussion of the origin of both Eastern and Western religions is necessary in order to fully appreciate the purpose of this book. We can look to the biography of the various saviors and prophets and note a common theme: poverty background, many struggles throughout their life, a high point of their message and ascension.

The ancient Mystery Schools were studied by the more significant religious figures, such as Krishna, Moses, Pythagoras, Rama, Orpheus, Plato, Hermes, Jesus and the Jewish Essenes.

When the white Aryan race migrated out of Central Asia and into Iran, India and the Far East at about 2000 B.C., they began a civilization composed of red, black, yellow and white races. This period of history was quite paternal. Only the prophets and rishis had the right to speak. Women lost the stature they held in Egypt, where they could become priestesses. Now men enslaved women and removed them from their religious groups.

European development allowed for a significant role for women in religious life. In Greece we find evidence of female oracles and prophetesses, such as the Greek Pythones. Women fought in Druid battles, and in certain tribes others attained the position of rulers.

When the white race later conquered the black European coastal societies, they later invaded North Africa and central Asia. The mixing of the black and white race during the iron age produced the Semitic people, which included the Jews, Arabs, Menes, Phoenicians, Chaldeans and Egyptians.

From the Middle East now came an overflowing of religious, scientific and philosophical thought. Among the results of this intellectual and spiritual explosion were the sacred scriptures of the Torah of the Jews, the New Testament of the Christians and the Islamic Koran.

In the East the sacred Hindu writings known as the Vedas arose from Aryan influence. Other sacred scriptures from this region were the Ramayana, the Zend-Avest and Buddha's teachings. It is through both the Aryan and Semitic writings that the great ideas of philosophy, art, mythology, science and religion flourished.

Herein lies one of the great conflicts in history. Both schools, Aryan and Semitic, professed the ultimate truth. Since their paradigms are quite divergent, religious wars and other dysfunctional forms of prejudice resulted. Let us explore these differences in the path to ascension.

The concept of unity and universality in the name of a supreme God was the message of the Semitic people. The Aryan paradigm claimed an ascending evolution from the mineral kingdom to plants, lower animals and man eventually to a spiritual heaven or nirvana.

For the Semites the Spirit emanates from God and descends into man. Man now becomes the Godman on Earth.

The opposite approach is offered by the Aryans, in which man's Spirit ascends to God until the soul becomes incorporated in the God complex.

Historically we can trace the Semitic religion back to Moses, approximately 3,300 years ago. About 2,000 years before Moses, the Aryan migration into India established the Eastern philosophies. The Semitic teachings of Moses were refined by Jesus so that the common man could relate to them. This led to the formation and eventual spread of Christianity, given credibility when officially sanctified by the Roman Empire during the fourth century A.D.

The Aryan religious beliefs spread eastward into Persia (Iran) and Greece. Eventually the northern countries of Europe became exposed to this theology. These opposing Semitic and Aryan ideas appear to be unreconcilable.

When we want life to do something for us we are demonstrating the dysfunctional principle of neediness. Asking God to supply us with material and spiritual things leads to frustration and failure more often than not. Now we are more vulnerable to turn to some form of religion as a type of codependency to obtain what we want.

The miracles we commonly seek do not manifest themselves commonly. Religions preach love, but don't really define it. Instructions are given by some religions to love regardless of what occurs in our lives.

Polarity seems to be ingrained in human nature. If the love concept doesn't meet our needs, we turn to its opposite, or hate. This hatred has, more than anything I can think of, fostered the majority of our woes. Whether it be jealousy, greed or other forms of insecurities, our violent and destructive nature has arisen from this principle of hate.

Since our struggles in life involve philosophical and religious components in our quest of divine knowledge, let us explore the differences in detail between the Eastern and Western religions. We will consider Animism, Buddhism, Christianity, Hinduism, Islamism, Jainism, Judaism, the Mystery Schools, Shintoism, Sufism, Taoism and Zoroastrianism. There are other theologies, but this survey will suffice in presenting an overview of religion's attempt to train us for ascension.

Animism

The term Animism was coined in 1871 by Edward B. Tylor. This theory implied that we all possess an immaterial and eternal soul. The data obtained from visions and dreams of primitive people represented the source of this theology.

In 1899 R. R. Marett proposed a refinement to the animism concept by stating that primitive man did not conceive of individual souls, but assumed that some form of force animated the body. He referred to this force as animatism. Marett further presented the supposition that primitive peoples merely acted out their religion, rather than planning out specific paradigms. He stated that it was more like the early examples of magical rites and ceremonies.

Animism is alleged to have developed into polytheism when these spirits were worshiped as gods. For example, we find the god of the woods represented by Silvanus, and Aeolus as the god of the winds. Eventually a supreme deity arose and polytheism evolved into monotheism, as expressed in Judaism, Christianity, Islamism and Zoroastrianism.

Buddhism

We have already discussed Buddhism at length in Chapter 2. For our purposes in this survey let me summarize its theology. Buddhism originates from the teachings of Siddhartha Gautama, who lived about 500 B.C. The Mahayana division emphasizes contemplation and salvation, whereas the Theravada branch preserves the early monastic writings.

Zen Buddhism originates from the Mahayana component and focuses on self-examination, gentleness and introspection. The Lamaistic division of Tibet combines more primitive paradigms with Buddhism proper.

Originally separating itself from Hinduism, Buddhism incorporates its concepts of enlightenment, or satori, and cosmic consciousness from its predecessor. Buddha has appeared from time to time throughout history, whenever people's knowledge of dharma is lost. There were reportedly 24 Buddhas who preceded Buddha Gautama.

Buddhism as preached by its founder was presented in the form of anecdotes, similes and parables. It was designed to encourage people to personally commit themselves to 'the path.' Only the individual could ascertain the truth. This philosophy has survived in modern practices of Buddhism. The only way to truly comprehend the doctrines of Buddha is to practice it regularly and with faith.

Christianity

The most identifiable religion in the Western world is Christianity. Saint Paul established this religion by spreading the teachings of Jesus as he understood it. Paul never knew Jesus, nor was he a follower of Christ in the beginning. The

New Testament contains the Gospels, which are based on the principles of right action and love. The individual who personally knew Jesus and was reportedly the bearer of Christ's spiritual heritage was Simon Peter.

The disciple Peter on the slopes of Mt. Hermon answered the question, "Who do men say that I am?" with the statement, "Thou are the Christ" (the Messiah).[1] This was a reference to the deliverer promised to the Jews in the Old Testament.

Thomas, another apostle, stated after Jesus' resurrection, "My Lord and my God."[2] Thomas initially doubted that Jesus had risen. We find in Christianity components of a supernatural religion and a sense of history.

Christianity preached specific purposes in creation: a redemption from evil and the salvation of the individual. This faith made many moral demands upon its followers and filled them with a new divine power, called the Holy Spirit.

This Holy Spirit represented an eternal life which began in the here-and-now and continued beyond the death of the physical body in a resurrected body. St. John summed it up best when he stated, "In the beginning was the Word and the Word was with God, and the Word was God . . . all things were made by him . . . In him was life; and the life was the light of men."[3]

---

[1] Matt. 24:13; Mark 8:29.

[2] John 20:28.

[3] John 1:1-4.

Hinduism

Most of the people of India practice Hinduism. This polytheistic theology worships three principal gods. This trinity of Shiva, Brahma and Vishnu is expressed in the scriptures known as the Vedas, which includes the Upanishads and Cosmic consciousness, or the enlightenment of the mental component of our being. The cults of Rama and Krishna (the reincarnation of Vishnu), Skanda, Ganesha and Dorga are but a few of the offshoots of Hinduism.

Of importance to our discussion of ascension is the Upanishads. This sacred text first describes three doctrines paramount in religious history. These doctrines are:

1. The principle that the soul is repeatedly reborn in a new body. This is called samsara.
2. Karmic doctrine states that we bear the effects of our deeds and actions in our present and future lifetimes.
3. The concept of Moksha declares that there is an end to the cycle of birth and death and rebirth. A state of nirvana signifies this ascension.

Another component of Hinduism is the principle of ahimsa or nonviolence. It is sinful to take the life of an animal or human under any circumstances. To do so results in a rebirth as a lower animal with much karma.

The worshipers of the god Shiva in the form of a stone lingam propose a mechanism of ascension based upon meditation, penance, periodic devotions and worship of the lingam. The avatra doctrine discusses how vision takes on an Earthly form to save the world from destruction by evil forces.

The ten avatars of Vishnu are:

1.   The Fish (Matsya)
2.   The Tortoise (Karma)
3.   The Boar (Varaha)
4.   The Man-Lion (Narasimha)
5.   The Dwarf (Vamana)
6.   Rama of the Axe (Parashu Rama)
7.   Rama, King of Adodhya
8.   Krishna
9.   The Buddha
10.   Kalkin, an incarnation of the future

Only Rama, Krishna and Buddha have survived in modern forms of Hinduism.

Islamism

Mohammad founded the Islamic religion during the seventh century A.D. The word Islam means having peace with God or submission to God. Five specific pillars of the Islamic faith are:

1.   The recital of their creed
2.   Praying facing the direction of Mecca five times a day
3.   Almsgiving
4.   Fasting in the month of Ramadan
5.   Pilgrimages to the Kaaba, the holy shrine located in the city of Mecca in Saudi Arabia

Mohammad received a series of angelic revelations that

were written down and preserved as the Koran over a period of more than 20 years. This 114-chapter sacred text is the same length as the New Testament. The Koran is believed by Muslims to be the very word of God.

The Koran is most definitely an original religious work, differing considerably from the Old Testament and New Testament. Mohammad was reportedly illiterate, and therefore unable to model his scripture from other sources.

Not a book of theology in the usual sense, the Koran is more of a religious rhetoric designed to instruct, warn and admonish. Conflicts abound concerning such concepts as free will and predestination. At times the scripture focuses on the complete control God has over human affairs, while at other instances it emphasizes our choice whether or not to obey God.

The Islamic belief is most definitely monotheistic. The Allah or God of the Muslims is a sole and unique sovereignty, as compared to the dualism of Zoroastrians, for example.

Jainism

Jainism began as a protest against the ritualism of Hinduism. The last of its great leaders or Tirthankaras was Vardhamana, who lived during the sixth century B.C. Asceticism and nonviolence toward all living creatures are its main principles. We have discussed the Jainist views on Karma in Chapter 2.

Jainists propose the concept that there is neither a beginning nor an end to the universe. It simply passes through an infinite number of cosmic cycles, each of which is divided into two alternate phases of ascent and descent. During these cycles there is a gradual rise and fall of human civilization.

During each of these phases 24 Tirthankaras appear. These leaders attain liberation for themselves and teach the art of ascension to others. The first of these 24 Tirthankaras during our current age of decline was Rishabha.

Jainists state that the nature of reality is characterized by a simultaneous operation of permanence, origination and destruction. The Jainist concept of soul is both finite and infinite. The soul acquires a new form in rebirth, but discards its old form. It remains eternal by not relinquishing its essential quality of spiritual evolution or consciousness.

Ascension for the Jainists is through an interminable line of Tirthankaras. These are not gods, as the Jainist philosophy is an atheistic one. All those who follow the path proposed by this religion are assured of eventual ascension and omniscience.

Judaism

The oldest reported monotheistic religion in the world is Judaism. The God Jehovah is worshiped as the Supreme Being for all orthodox Jews. The Torah (the first of five books of the Old Testament), the remainder of the Old Testament and the Talmud (a collection of later interpretations and Jewish teachings) summarize the creed and experiences of the Jews dating back some 3,500 years.

The name Jehovah often assigned to the Jewish God is a medieval misreading and does not appear in the Old Testament. The names of the Lord that do appear in the scriptures are Shaddai, El*ah, Yah, Adonai, Elohim and Yhuh.

The Hebrew God is a demanding, remote and transcendent being, who demands absolute obedience under the sanction of severe penalties. The Lord is also portrayed as a compassionate and loving creature who has a close and personal relationship with those who worship Him.

Jewish prophets were men who believed to be specifically summoned by God to relay his message. According to Judaism, God created humans with free will to choose between good and evil. It is through revelations that God communicates with man. We can contact the Lord through meditation and prayer.

Ascension can be accomplished through fulfillment of the Torah. As all people are considered equal, we are not born with an inherited burden of sin. Judaism preaches a world-affirming, not a world-denying faith.

Traditional Judaism states that we are born in a good world created by God. The emphasis is placed on the care of body and soul in this world, rather than focusing on preparation for eternity.

Ascension is heralded by the arrival of a personal Messiah, who is human and descended from the house of David. In the Torah we find 248 positive and 365 negative commandments (mitzvot). A mitzvah is an expression of God's will, and is binding on the believing Jew. By living a life in accord with divine will, a bearing of witness to God and His purpose in the world is established, and ascension is assured.

The Cabala is the mysticism teachings of the Jews concerning Jehovah. This doctrine comprises metaphysical speculations and mystical interpretations of Jewish scripture. It is divided into theoretical and practical components. The theoretical doctrines are concerned with both literal and dogmatic approaches. The practical division comprises instruction in amulets and talismans. It must be noted that the Cabala is based on mathematics and is the basis of all techniques of magic.

Spiritual exercises, such as contemplation and meditation, is recommended as the path to personal union with God. I alluded to the mathematical basis of the Cabala. The world was created by means of the 22 letters and ten numbers of the Hebrew language. The Cabala survives today through the emergence of the Hasidic sect, which was founded by Baal Shem Tov during the eighteenth century.

The Mystery Schools

The term Mystery Schools refers to the policy of the priests of this ancient religion keeping secret from the masses the basis of this pagan theology that would impart advantages to the initiate on bettering their current life and achieving ascension.

Throughout Greece, Egypt, and the Roman empire, this religion dominated until the rise of Christianity. Women were excluded from their rituals. Through seven stages of advancement, symbolizing the journey of the soul after physical death through the seven heavens into the God realm, the initiate, or catechumen, was guided by a hierophant, who assisted them in this quest.

The ultimate purpose of the mysteries was enlightenment and direct experience with the Absolute. By purifying the soul through a raising of consciousness, the initiate prepared himself for his eventual ascension.

Mystery rituals involved sacrifices and prayer. The five components of a typical ritual were as follows:

First was the preliminary purification; second, the mystic communication, which included an exhortation; third, a revelation transpired; fourth, the initiate was crowned with a garland; and finally, a state of fulfillment resulting from communion with the deity was achieved. Dancing was included in all mystery ceremonies.

Avoiding the dangers that confronted the soul after physical death was established by providing the initiate with rules and techniques. Magic formulas were taught to repel demons. This is well documented in the *Egyptian Book of the Dead*, among other sources.

It is suggested by many scholars that the mysteries provided a model for Christianity. The Christian concept of resurrection of the body was taken from the history of the Egyptian god Osiris, who was killed and dismembered but arose as a resurrected body. The Indian mysteries with their trinity of three main gods may also have inspired the Christian trinity.

Shintoism

Shintoism is an ancient Japanese religion that consists of a set of customs and rituals involving festivals, shrines and the worship of several gods. Buddhism exerted a great influence on this religion.

Bodily cleanliness and ceremonial life are the heart of Shintoism. There is no moral or ethical system to speak of. A sun goddess was the main deity until approximately the seventh century when the emperor became the revered symbol. Following World War II Shintoism divested itself of its previous tendency to glorify the militaristic philosophy of the government. The emperor was stripped of his divine status at that time.

Shintoism is a difficult religion for the Westerner to relate to. Its emphasis is on intuitiveness with greater emphasis on religious experience than on the reasoning out of theological concepts.

For Shintoists, feeling the reality of the Kami (god) providing a direct experience of divinity and a recognition of the mystery of eventual ascension are more important than an intellectual approach to theology.

Sufism

Sufism is Islamic mysticism. Its objective is to attain union with God. Through suppression of the ego, an immediate experience of the divine is possible, and eventually ascension. Revelation is the deeper spiritual meaning that can only be attained by those who have been instructed in its secrets by Sufi masters.

The exoteric and esoteric levels of religious knowledge are symbolic, with every rule of shariah pointing to a higher truth that indicates one of the paths (tariqah) to God or ascension.

Fana is the extinction of the individuality in the reality of God. When one achieves fana only God is seen. This is a state of ecstasy in which all human attributes are left aside. Although fana is temporary, baqa, in an enduring condition of complete union with God or ascension to keep oneself free of worldly corruption, self-mortification or zund, is practiced.

Taoism

The Chinese mysticism is represented by Taoism. This

theology obtained knowledge of God and the universe in the trance-state of the shaman, rather than in ancient scripture. There are three works that make up this mystical religion: the Chung Tzu, Lieh Tzu and the Tao Tê Ching (The Way and Its Power). The latter work is credited to the Chinese philosopher Lao Tzu. Only an adept can know the "greater knowledge." He gains this awareness in trance during which "I lose me." During his trance the adept goes on a shamanic journey "riding upon the wind" borne by "cloud chariots" to God. The adept envisions Heaven and Earth as being created by God together with man. All things are considered as one.

All things are viewed as relative to the Taoist. All contrasts are harmonized as the One is Tao. Tao can do everything by doing nothing. Human interference in this system is always damaging. The adept opposes all moral laws, institutions and government.

Happiness and eventual ascension are achieved by allowing Tao free-play. What is, is good. Engaging in actionless activities assures eternal life. Death is merely an exchange of one existence for another.

Zoroastrianism

The religion developed in eastern Persia (Iran) by Zarathustra (who later became known as Zoroaster) during the sixth century B.C. is called Zoroastrianism. The Zend Avesta is its sacred text. Modern forms of this religion survive as the Parsis of India.

The main theme of this theology addresses the ethical and dualistic struggle between good and evil or light and darkness.

Zoroastrianism coincided with the conversion of Persian people from a primitive to a cultured environment. The Order of the Magi arose out of this religion and came to be known as the Wise Men of the East.

God to the Zoroastrians is the Wise Lord Ahura Mazda, who created Heaven and Earth. The Evil Spirit opposes this god. We humans have the free choice either to follow the path of evil or that of truth. Ascension is the ultimate result of following the path of truth.

Matter is not evil to the Zoroastrians. The devil or Evil Spirit is alien to the material world. This negative force attempts to destroy God's work. Zoroastrianism is a joyful religion.

There is a judgment of the soul following death. Ascension results if the good outweighs the bad. If this criterion is not met, the soul is sent to hell. This is only a temporary punishment, as on the day of resurrection God purifies all souls and destroys the devil. At this time all souls achieve ascension.

Figure 1 illustrates this wheel of ascension as composed of the various religions we discussed.

The main purpose of all religions is to prepare us for ascension. Unfortunately, their success rate isn't very impressive. The fact that we reincarnate over and over again illustrates this failure. Furthermore, society's degeneration of moral, social and spiritual values, accompanied by its addiction to materialism, only adds to my thesis. We must look within ourselves to attain soul liberation and ascension.

Fig. 1   The Wheel of Ascension

Chapter 4:

_____ *Raising Your Consciousness*

*I*t is absolutely necessary for us to raise our consciousness to
ascend into the higher planes to join God. My concept of
ascension is one of being a co-worker with God. This differs
considerably from the Hindu paradigm of being absorbed into
the God energy as a passive component.

To truly ascend is to become quite active in the ultimate
spiritual journey. Freedom of choice and determination of this
path is most definitely a part of our eternal reward. The main
temptation that can prevent this spiritual evolution is obsession
with the material world. The only way I know of to overcome
this attachment is by raising our consciousness.

We must always remember that our individual embodiment has three components. These are the body, mind, and
spirit or soul. In body we seek happiness in a more physical,
sometimes sensual manner. Within mind there is another type
of seeking and volition through thought. Our spirit utilizes
action and awareness in its quest for fulfillment. The soul is
basically a happy entity, so living within our spirit is a path to
happiness.

The state of ascension will be attained through working
within our natural and eternal state of consciousness we call the
subconscious. One of the effects of raising our consciousness

61

into a more spiritual level is an elimination of a need to seek. We will continue to seek the truth and spiritual perfection, but not from a needy perspective.

Practicing the exercises in this book is one way to facilitate your consciousness growth. This must be done over a period of years to achieve the goal on which this book is based. The sooner you begin, the quicker and greater will be your rewards.

Consciousness is considered as one in the spiritually evolved soul. The Hindus referred to it as unity. We all seek our own level of this consciousness, but it must be raised to savor the rewards of an eternal life of bliss. Few of us accept the concept that we exist as one.

A form of self-recognition is created when we finally realize what *is*. There is no reality outside of our consciousness. Our subconscious creates all that we perceive through our five senses.

This consciousness we call our own is manifested in whatever form we desire ourselves to be. We and only our desires and direction shape our states of consciousness. This is why it is critical to develop a right moral and ethical attitude and code of behavior during our physical sojourn on the physical plane.

Once we maintain this connection with our Higher Self, then we can free ourselves from the tyranny of the belief that causes outside ourselves affect us. Since consciousness is spirit, the world we live in is an infinite number of consciousness. The worlds or planes beyond the physical that I will present in Chapter 5 are merely a continuation of these countless levels of consciousness.

The process of both accessing and joining our Higher Self leads to a recognition that we are never separated from the God energy. Our Higher Self is an extension of this God energy that is at our disposal for advice, comfort and spiritual growth at any time we choose.

One problem I consistently observe among my patients is a complaint about the state of their current lives. Each one of us chooses our own states of consciousness to function. These various states are nothing but quantum potentials until we enter them and become one with them. Herein lies one of the great secrets of life: We can improve the state of consciousness we observe by entering into a level of awareness we desire and becoming one with it.

In order to dwell with God we must live each day with the mind set that this is our reality and destiny. It is this form of knowingness that makes this goal attainable. We must direct and discipline our subconscious mind through various exercises to bring about this raise in consciousness.

The principle of psychic empowerment can never be overemphasized. Spirit is the true underlying cause of all effects we observe. We must eliminate dependency on any person, place, thing or paradigm that detours us from our spiritual path. Our Higher Self is the inner force that will shape and direct our lives in a manner allowing us to take charge of our world and raise our consciousness simultaneously.

It would be nice and simple to assume that your high-quality behavior would be returned in kind by others. Unfortunately, the negative forces in our world outweigh the positive ones. For example, love by itself will not beget love. We need only to look at the life of Jesus to illustrate this point.

Jesus preached love and lived this principle as an ideal model. However, he was not universally loved. In fact, he was hated by many of his fellow Jews for stirring up so much trouble with the Romans. This further upsetting of the social structure of the Jews resulted in much hatred by many of them, and his eventual crucifixion.

I am not advocating a withdrawal of love from your behavior. Non-attachment from the material world and psychic empowerment is what I am recommending. Nor am I advocating a state of asceticism, in which all material things are rejected and one's thoughts are solely directed to think only of God.

It is quite possible to accept your social, financial and other responsibilities, while at the same time remaining detached from the aspects of the material world that retard our spiritual growth. We can accomplish this by way of the superconscious mind tap I will shortly present.

The spiritual unfoldment of the soul and degree of its awakened consciousness is different for each of us. That is why we are all different in our level of spiritual evolvement. When our soul is still imperfect at the time of our physical death, it spends a certain amount of time on what we describe as the soul plane prior to its rebirth.

The past history of our soul is not really important. We may have lived as a hardened criminal, prostitute or just an average person. All that matters is we begin to raise our consciousness and progress toward God-Realization. In establishing a path toward God, we must learn to discriminate between choices that will facilitate ascension versus those that only function to distract us from our ultimate goal.

Love as a unifying principle must be emphasized. This love is an adhesive force that binds our universe together. The doctrine of universal unity implies our identifying and merging with the love of God.

All things in our realm are governed by this love principle. When Moses said, "I AM THAT I AM" while standing before the burning bush representing God, he meant that the individuality within each of us is able to separate itself and become its own pure spirit. All things are of the same divine essence we call God, and Ascension is our path back to this Source.

The characteristics of a raised consciousness is difficult to describe to those who are enmeshed in the material world. This movement of our inner consciousness through lower states until it ascends into states of ecstasy is exemplified by an absolute awareness of being.

The soul is now moving with regions of space and time to areas beyond these concepts. It is here that a total omniscient presence is felt in the form of total awareness. It is from this level that we are able to reach a perfected state and ascend. To do this we must saturate ourselves with a spiritual ideal and meld the mind and body with our soul.

We will observe many positive changes along this path. Some of the most notable occurrences are a loss of tendencies for exhibiting vanity, anger, bigotry, impatience, possessiveness, intolerance, laziness, cruelty, faultfinding, cravings for alcohol and other drugs and attachment to the material world.

To foster this path of spiritual growth we must develop a love for all that lives. This universal love applies to those who do us kind or unkind acts. This love surpasses all human understanding, as it eliminates the tendency for vengeance or other dysfunctional aspects of an insecure soul.

In our spiritual growth we must learn to recognize the transient nature of the physical world. The soul is permanent and cannot be harmed in life or death. Regardless of life's setbacks, we must discipline ourselves to rise above material attachments.

The actions of our deeds are more important than the results obtained. Becoming indifferent to pain, anxiety, fear, passion and anger will foster our spiritual evolution. Most people become involved with spiritual techniques and paradigms after much search and frustration because of their inability to practice these very principles.

It is suggested that we detach ourselves in our innermost feelings from involvement in the aspects of our daily lives that detour us from our spiritual path. By losing our affection and needy attachment to our environment and possessions, we become independent of them and well on our way to ascension.

At all times I am stressing the maintenance of our freedom and independence in our quest for nirvana. When you die, all that you will bring with you to the next world is your soul. Your possessions, physical body, emotions and other Earthly attachments remain on the physical plane.

Western society does not promote often or well the concept of giving without expectation of reward. This form of unselfish giving as an aspect of unconditional love is one of the earliest steps to perfection of our soul.

This process of self-purification involves refraining from trying to reform others. Our humility is fostered and we begin to detach ourselves from material things. This detachment is often one of the last steps in freeing our soul from the bondage of the karmic cycle.

We must also resist the temptation to blame others for our problems. It is always within our own consciousness that we can find both the origin and solution of any difficulty we can define.

It is desire that overwhelms the soul and retards its spiritual unfolding. Our senses are the source of desire. Our mind will continually use this desire principle as an excuse to repeat past dysfunctional cravings if left unchecked. The resulting karma acts to delay our eventual ascension.

By allying with the God energy, as manifested by our Higher Self, we will find attainable the path to liberation of our soul. Attachment to material things and people, all of which are temporary, acts to bind us to the wheel of karma.

The tendency to express fear that we will lose our possessions makes it impossible to attain the state of ascension. Eliminating our attachment to the physical world is not easy, and we can see why it is commonly the last lesson to be mastered prior to the soul's perfection.

All things become possible when we achieve this desireless state. The initial step toward this goal can be attained by accessing our Higher Self. The technique I developed in 1977 to do this is called the superconscious mind tap.

Here is a self-hypnosis script of this method. As with all the techniques I present in this book, I suggest making a tape of this script. You can contact my office to obtain my recorded tape of this method.

Superconscious Mind Tap

Begin this exercise with a standard relaxation technique. Chapter 13 will cover this in greater detail.

Now listen very carefully. I want you to imagine a bright white light coming down from above and entering the top of your head. Filling your entire body. See it, feel it and it becomes reality. Now imagine an aura of pure white light emanating from your heart region. Again surrounding your entire body. Protecting you. See it, feel it and it becomes reality. Now only your Masters and Guides and highly evolved loving entities who mean you well will be able to influence you during this or any other hypnotic session. You are totally protected by this aura of pure white light.

In a few moments I am going to count from 1 to 20. As I do so you will feel yourself rising up to the superconscious mind level where you will be able to receive information from your Masters and Guides. You will also be able to overview all of your past, present and future lives. Number 1 rising up. 2, 3, 4 rising higher. 5, 6, 7, letting information flow. 8, 9, 10, you are halfway there. 11, 12, 13, feel yourself rising even higher. 14, 15, 16, almost there. 17, 18, 19, number 20 you are there. Take a moment and orient yourself to the superconscious mind level.

Play New Age Music for 1 Minute

You may now ask yourself any question about any past, present or life issue. Or, you may contact any of your guides or departed loved ones from this level. You may explore your relationship with any person. Remember, your superconscious mind level is all knowledgeable and has access to your akashic records. Now slowly and carefully state your desire for information or an experience and let this superconscious mind level work for you.

Play New Age Music for 8 Minutes

You have done very well. Now I want you to further open up the channels of communication by removing any obstacles and allowing yourself to receive information and experiences that will directly apply to and help better your present lifetime. Allow yourself to receive more advanced and more specific information from your Higher Self and Masters and Guides to raise your frequency and improve your karmic subcycle. Do this now.

Play New Age Music for 8 Minutes

Alright now. Sleep now and rest. You did very very well. Listen very carefully. I'm going to count forward now from 1–5. When I reach the count of 5 you will be back in the present, you will be able to remember everything you experienced and re-experienced, you'll feel very relaxed, refreshed, you'll be able to do whatever you have planned for the rest of the day or evening. You'll feel very positive about what you've just experienced and very motivated about your confidence and ability to play this tape again to experience the superconscious mind level. Alright now. 1 very very deep, 2 you're getting a little bit lighter, 3 you're getting much much lighter, 4 very very light, 5 awaken. Wide awake and refreshed.

The link with the Higher Self was expressed nicely by George Russell as follows:

"Some self of me, higher in the tower of being which reaches up to the heavens, made objective manifestation of its thought; but there were moments when it seemed itself to descend, wrapping its memories of heaven about it like a cloth, and to enter the body, and I knew it more truly myself than that which began in my mother's womb, and that it was antecedent to anything which had my body in the world."[1]

The metaphysical writer Dion Fortune commented on this state of awareness with equal vigor:

"I could not so desire what was not my own. . . . When the Higher Self and the lower self become united through the complete absorption of the lower by the higher, true adepthood is gained; this is the Great Initiation, the lesser Divine Union. It is the supreme experience of the incarnate soul."[2]

Spiritual Protection

Before presenting exercises on consciousness raising, it is important to apply psychic protection. A thorough discussion of this concept, along with over 60 exercises, is presented in my book Protected by the Light.

Psychic attacks may seem the material horror movies are made of, but let me assure you they are quite real. Every one of us is exposed to psychic attacks throughout our daily lives. Our only protection is the energy shield surrounding our physical body known as the aura. This psychic assault comprises political and religious appeals, threats of violence, noise pollution, news of crime, guilt, fear, advertisements and many other factors.

Our makeup is multidimensional. We have physical, mental, emotional and spiritual facets to our beings that operate simultaneously. In order for psychic protection to be

---

[1] George Russell, "The Candle of Vision" (Dorset: Prism Press, 1990).
[2] Dion Fortune, "The Mystical Qabalah (York Beach, Maine: Samuel Weiser, 1984), p. 291.

established, these factors must be aligned and balanced. Whatever the mind can create, it can uncreate. These psychic attacks are a creation of mind energy.

It is imperative that you strengthen your aura and reduce your exposure to these precipitating factors as much as possible to prevent such an attack. By using the approaches presented here, you will be able to prevent such an insult, or eliminate one already initiated, and even extend this shielding effect to your family, workplace and community.

Invisible forces exist in our everyday lives. Some of these energies are beneficial to our health and well being, while others literally attack the core of our existence. The average person in his or her normal life is exposed to paranormal forces that attack the psyche. A psychic attack is quite serious. Feelings of guilt, anger, sadness or fear can be brought on from this type of assault. We may overreact to many ordinary life situations.

The afflicted individual is usually unaware of the cause of these disturbances. Physicians are stumped, since all their traditional tests come out negative. Most therapists find these patients frustrating, and are unequipped to handle them. These people are misdiagnosed and given antidepressants or other prescriptions which are quite ineffective against the symptoms exhibited by the psychic attack.

Any emotional imbalance may lower our resistance and allow for a psychic attack to occur. It is the energy imbalance of our soul that causes this emotional vulnerability in the first place. Anything we can do to raise the quality of our soul's energy will build up our emotional and physical immune system. Our aura will be strengthened and no psychic attack will be possible.

Love is always the key to health and psychic protection. Any expression of nonlove toward yourself will cause an imbalance that will make you more susceptible to these attacks. When you criticize or condemn yourself, express doubts concerning your decisions or actions, tell yourself that you are too fat, old or short, you are priming the pump for a psychic attack.

The most common form of spiritual shielding is in the form of a white light protection.[3] In addition to protecting you against the influence of negative entities, these techniques neutralize distracting and uncomfortable subconscious and conscious thoughts and feelings about yourself and others. You will note that I included a white light protection in my superconscious mind tape script.

Try this centering and balancing exercise to acquaint yourself with this approach:

1.   Relax, breathe deeply and imagine a bright white light located with your own heart. This light allows you to access your Higher Self.

2.   Mentally visualize this light vibrating at a rapid rate and permeating every fiber of your physical body.

3.   Each breath you inhale magnifies this spreading of this light throughout your body. This light becomes even more intense as you exhale.

4.   Keep focusing on your breathing and perceive a feeling of love and strength surrounding your body and merging with your aura.

---

[3] B. Goldberg, "Protected by the Light: The Complete Book of Psychic Self-Defense" (Tucson, AZ: Hats Off Books, 2000).

To add to this effect of protection from outside psychic attack, practice this approach:

1. Relax, breathe deeply and surround your entire body with a white light.
2. Perceive this white light taking the form of a thick shield surrounding your body, which immediately neutralizes and dissolves any negativity that attempts to enter your awareness.
3. Use your breathing imagery described in the previous exercise to strengthen this shielding effect.

Try this protection exercise to facilitate raising your consciousness:

1. Relax and sit in a comfortable chair. Close your eyes and visualize yourself entering the very depths of your soul.
2. Guide your soul in the direction of a white light located in the center of your being. You will feel a pull of energy. Merge with this energy.
3. Sense any vibrations, sounds and colors. Observe them but do not analyze them. Refrain from becoming emotional. Pay particular attention to any sensations on your neck and face. Feel rejuvenated as a result.
4. Visualize gold rays of light taking the form of threads spinning around your body. These threads are lifting you up and freeing your soul from the inhibitions of the physical body and the conscious mind.
5. Perceive things differently now. You have just

increased your spiritual vision. You can hear and feel things better at this time.

6.   Move your arms and legs to allow this charged life energy to move all throughout your physical body. Feel the freedom of your healing energy and your soul. Enjoy these sensations and encourage these feelings.

7.   Visualize the white light entering and surrounding your entire body. This white light is filled with your healing energy.

8.   Step back into your physical body as you imagine the golden threads gently lowering your very essence back to your physical awareness. Slowly stretch your body, take deep breaths and open your eyes.

The Garden Meditation for Raising Consciousness

We will thoroughly discuss meditation in Chapter 8. The exercise I am about to present is a very simple, yet effective, technique to assist you in raising your consciousness.

Since every aspect of our physical experience has its counterpart in thought, our thoughts reflect our experience and the experience we perceive is the result of our thoughts. The garden meditation is a fascinating mechanism for initiating growth and change. It is a method of organizing our thoughts into a specific pattern that creates new understanding about our current circumstances.

To begin this approach simply take a few deep breaths and allow your body to relax. Mentally create an image of a garden in your mind's eye. Make it as real as you can. Your initial attempts to create this garden may result in vague outlines or unclear images. You might not receive a visual image at all.

Do not be concerned about this.

You can facilitate this technique by selecting a quiet and relaxing environment where you will be undisturbed for 15 to 30 minutes. With practice and experience, you will be able to initiate this procedure anywhere and at any time.

For a specific technique try this:

1. Close your eyes and take a deep breath. Hold it for as long as you can and let it out slowly. Repeat this a second time and let the image of a garden enter your mind.

2. Now direct your attention to visualize three objects (a tree, an animal and a flower, for example); touch three elements of this scene (grass, tree, a butterfly); and hear three things (a bird chirping, the wind, a babbling brook).

3. Spend some time walking through this garden. Note the landscape, the flowers, trees, insects, sounds and smells of your creation. Find a reference point that will function as your sanctuary, or place of peace and tranquillity. This may be a lake or cave or place under a tree.

4. Since everything in your life is reflected and represented in your garden, we are going to use this vehicle to raise your consciousness.

5. Return to your sanctuary and ask the garden to give you information about improving your life, finding out your karmic purpose and raising your consciousness. This garden is a magical place and functions according to its own natural laws. You may converse with the birds,

trees, rocks, flowers or spirit guides here. Spend a few moments in this dialogue and meditate on the information you receive.

6.   Now invite your spirit guide to assist you. Simply make this request in your sanctuary for this guide to appear. Ask your Higher Self to select only a positive and spiritually advanced guide to appear. You may request for a specific guide, such as a relationship or health guide.

7.   When your guide appears greet him or her and ask your questions. Listen intently and keep your objectivity. Your guide should offer advice, but always leave the final action or choice up to you. Dismiss this guide if it attempts to tell you what to do or orders you to engage in any unethical behavior.

8.   This guide may appear as a human animal, extraterrestrial or mythological character.

9.   Following the conclusion of this communication, spend some additional time in your sanctuary. Request your Higher Self to assist you in raising your consciousness. Meditate in this state for an additional five minutes.

10.   After this procedure, bless your garden and Higher Self and return to your physical awareness. Take two deep breaths and open your eyes.

This garden meditation can be used at any time you feel tense or just want to relax. You may shorten this procedure to just five minutes for this recharging purpose.

It is not unusual to have an out-of-body experience (OBE) with this exercise. Changes in your garden may be observed as you grow spiritually. By making a regular trip to your garden you can overview your current level of growth and facilitate healthy changes.

For example, if you notice elements of this garden that require attention (dying plants, dry soil, weeds, the presence of litter), then you can take the appropriate steps and make the improvement indicated. As you attend to your garden in your mind, the equivalent positive changes will be noted in your consciousness, as it is raised.

Any problem you are facing in your physical plane life can be solved by returning to your garden. These can be physical, mental, emotional or spiritual issues. The solutions to these problems very often manifest spontaneously. Sometimes they appear as very clear messages, and in other instances these answers to your questions will be represented by symbols.

When practicing the garden meditation, do not be concerned about the quality of your experience. We all have different methods of applying these approaches. Be patient and develop your visualization and concentration abilities. Chapters 6, 8, and 13 will assist you in this endeavor.

This technique, as are the others presented in later chapters, are merely tools to assist you in raising your consciousness. You may modify these approaches or create your own to deal with your individual circumstances. The only thing in the universe that you have direct exposure to that cannot be changed is your Higher Self, which represents the perfect component of your soul's energy.

There may be times when you run into monsters, demons or other negative entities in your garden, especially in your dream state. The white light protection techniques presented in this book will provide all the safety you need.

Your fears and insecurities are what create these negative images. You have the ability to destroy these monsters and transform them into allies. My book *Astral Voyages*[4] fully discusses techniques to accomplish this.

Here are two clinical examples of how my patients have used this method to deal with current issues:

1.   A woman in her late thirties complained about her frustrating and loveless marriage to her high school sweetheart. In her garden image she saw a large plant with withering leaves. When she asked it how she could improve her life the plant responded, "Just as I need water and fertilizer to grow and become healthy, your marriage requires patience, love and understanding to grow." My patient then applied both fertilizer and water to this dying plant from pails labeled patience, love and understanding. Subsequent to this experience her marriage improved and so did her attitude toward life in general.

2.   One of my male patients presented himself with an issue of professional frustration. No matter what he did, his chances for advancement in his job always seemed to be blocked. His garden was dominated by weeds and unwanted vegetation covered with thorns. He could not remove these objects himself, so he hired a group of gardeners to assist him in their removal.

This team thoroughly removed these plants by their roots, replowed the soil and planted vegetables labeled strength,

---

[4] B. Goldberg, "Astral Voyages: Mastering the Art of Soul Travel" (St. Paul: Llewellyn, 1998).

courage, confidence and prosperity. Two months later he received the first of several promotions.

In raising our consciousness we need to understand that its three levels need to work in harmony. The conscious mind proper, or willpower, represents our defense mechanisms and is quite resistant to change. We refer to our soul or spirit as the subconscious mind, which functions as a computer memory bank and is the part of our consciousness that reincarnates from life to life.

In order to perfect the subconscious so that we may be in a position to ascend, the cooperation of the Higher Self, or superconscious mind, must be attained. This Higher Self is our perfect energy remnant from the God energy we all came from. The superconscious mind tap is a way of exposing our subconscious to this Higher Self for the purpose of raising the former's frequency vibrational rate. A raise in consciousness results.

This concept of our superconscious mind being a form of personal god within does not in any way negate the usefulness of praying to Buddha, Allah, Jesus, Krishna or any other gods or goddesses of the various religions. All this implies is that your own Higher Self will be your agent either transmitting communication to God or receiving instructions from Him.

You are never alone, as your Higher Self is always with you. Even during our dream state this superconscious mind communicates with us through these nightly images to keep us updated as to our spiritual progress and sometimes gives us foreknowledge of things to come. There are telepathic dreams that come from people we know in this dream dimension, and even from situations that involve people we don't know. All of this data is first screened by our Higher Self.

During the day the conscious mind is more or less in control, and this physical dimension is perceived through the sensory information passed on by our subconscious. When we go to sleep, our subconscious gradually ceases to present the data from this dimension and begins to present data from another dimension. This other dimension does not have the same properties as the one we are more familiar with consciously. We will discuss this astral plane in Chapter 5.

Our Higher Self is composed of perfect energy. Ascension is actually the process of the merging of our subconscious mind with its Higher Self. The conscious mind dies when the physical body dies. Only the subconscious and superconscious survive physical death. Raising our consciousness as outlined in this chapter represents the first step toward ascension.

Always remember in your quest for spiritual growth that no person or entity can program your subconscious to control your thinking against your will. Unless drugs and sensory deprivation techniques are utilized, the best a person can do is attempt to influence our behavior or actions. Even though we live in a telepathic sea of feelings, thoughts and psychic energy, our free will is always functioning to screen out and censor this psychic garbage. Our Higher Self is also continually present to protect and advise us. It was the Greek philosopher Epictetus who stated, "Man is not disturbed about things, but by his opinion about things." Let us all remember this and from this day on take charge of our own lives and raise our consciousness.

Universal Laws

Although there are dozens of universal laws, I will summarize what I feel are the most important ones. Since these universal laws (truths) represent the main difference between religion and spirituality, let us discuss them:

1.   The Law of Free Will.
      Since the soul always has free will, it is our decision to be born at a certain time and place. It is our decision to choose our parents, friends, lovers, and enemies. We cannot blame other people or a bad childhood or marriage for our present problems. We are directly responsible for our lives because we have chosen the environment. The basic framework of your new life will be preplanned by you, but you can't plan every situation. Not only does your soul have free will, but so do all the souls that you will come into contact with in this new life. The main point there is that you choose the tests.

Although many of the major events in your life are laid out by you on the soul plane prior to your birth, you have free will to sidestep your destiny. Also, you always have free will in how you respond to any situation. If you respond with love, compassion and integrity, you have probably learned your karmic lesson and will not have to repeat the experience in the future.

We alone have the power to choose good over evil and growth over stagnation or degeneration. Only you can facilitate your spiritual growth and perfect your soul. Never blame any person, place or thing for your lot in life. It is free will that caused our fall from grace originally.

2.   The Law of Grace
        Karma can be experienced to the letter of the law or in mercy and grace. Wisdom erases karma. If you show mercy, grace and love, you will receive the same in return. This is also known as the principle of forgiveness. If you eliminate a negative behavior or weakness now, you erase all previous karma debts and don't have to work out any past life carryovers with every individual you may have wronged in the past, or who may have hurt you in previous existences.

3.   The Law of Challenge
        The universe never presents us with opportunities we cannot handle. You may be emotionally or physically overwhelmed, but not spiritually. Each obstacle and reward is place in our path to both challenge us and facilitate our growth as a soul.

4.   The Law of Karma
        This law focuses on cause and effect. For every action there is a reaction. Nothing happens by mere chance. We select the framework, including all obstacles and rewards, on the soul plane prior to our birth. Since we choose all of these lessons, there is nobody else to blame for our circumstances. "To thine own self be true."

All of our actions, particularly our motives, have

consequences. If you follow universal laws you will perfect the soul and ascend, as wisdom erases karma. If you continue repeating mistakes and fail lessons (you choose those lessons on the soul plane), you are asking for a long and frustrating karmic cycle of many dysfunctional lives.

5.   The Law of Attraction
      Like attracts like. Whatever you focus your energy on you will attract. If you are negative, you draw in and experience negativity. If you are loving, you draw in and experience love.

6.   The Law of Resistance
      You tend to attract those individuals and karmic lessons which you have resisted. This is a "mirror of karma" law.

7.   The Law of Divine Flow
      By accessing our Higher Self (superconscious mind), we are functioning as a channel for the energy complex and can accelerate our spiritual growth at a rapid rate. This law also explains how miracles occur.

8.   The Law of Polarity
      Everything has an opposite on the physical plane. These opposites (left, right, up, down, love, fear, good, evil, hot, cold, etc.) are identical in composition but only differ in direction or degree. This law is the foundation for the dual aspects of our world.

9.   The Law of Reciprocity
        The more you give, the more you will receive. The
        more you assist others, the more you assist yourself.

10.   The Law of Manifestation
        Our mind, not our brain, creates the material world we
        live. Quantum physics demonstrates how this
        mechanism works mathematically. Be careful for what
        you desire— it may very well come true.

11.   The Law of Consciousness
        Our consciousness (soul) is constantly expanding and
        thereby creating more opportunities for our spiritual
        growth. We can also lengthen our karmic cycle if we
        fail to follow universal laws.

12.   The Law of Abundance
        It is our mind (consciousness) that creates abundance.
        Through self-hypnosis and visualization techniques we
        can attract money, relationships, fame, better
        communication, spirituality and other goals into our
        reality.

13.   The Law of Correspondence
        This principle deals with what is known as the "mirror
        of karma." "As above so below" also applies here.
        The outer world (macrocosm) we live in is a reflection
        of the inner world (microcosm) of our consciousness.
        All objects created on the physical plane have a
        counterpart on the Astral plane. This law helps to

establish an interconnectedness between all components of our universe.

14. The Law of the Present Moment
     We live in a space-time continuum in which the past,
     present and future occurs simultaneously. It is only
     within our mind that we limit ourselves to the concepts
     of linear time. In reality, all that exists is in the present
     moment. In the higher planes, where all souls are
     perfect, this is referred to as the "Eternal Now."

15. The Law of Cycles
     As we discussed with the law of polarity, our universe
     is characterized by cycles. Day becomes night, winter
     ends and spring begins and whatever rises, eventually
     falls and rises again. This principle helps explain how
     our universe began (big bang) and will eventually
     collapse and rise again in a 40-billion year cyclic
     pattern.

16. The Law of Reincarnation
     This law is also known as the wheel of reincarnation or
     law of cyclic return. As long as we have lessons to
     learn (karma), our soul will be required to reincarnate
     into a body. It is only when perfection of the soul is
     achieved that this seemingly endless cycle is terminated
     and our soul merges with our Higher Self to ascend into
     the higher planes to reunite with God.

Summarizing Universal Laws

- We contain the power and energy of God in the form of our Higher Self. Unless we allow someone power over us, no other person can truly determine our destiny.

- We create our own reality through our thoughts, desires, feelings, attitudes, fears, beliefs, expectations and actions. Our world can and will change when we alter our thinking.

- We all contain the capability in the present moment to change any limiting beliefs and custom design our destiny. No past experience or perceived future can limit our spiritual growth unless we allow it to.

- The energy of the universe moves in the direction we select. Positive outlooks result in empowered futures, and cynical attitudes manifest as unnecessary struggles.

- The universe and all humans exist foremost because of love. When we acknowledge this principle we are both happy and moving closer to our eventual ascension.

- There is no absolute or ultimate truth. Truth lies in our own consciousness and level of spiritual evolvement.

*M*any of us assume that the physical plane we currently reside on is our only choice for our existence. Theology does talk about purgatory, heaven and hell, but does not detail other dimensions for our spiritual evolvement.

In this chapter we will overview the 13 planes that I originally described in my first book.[1] These planes are divided into the lower 5 planes (in which our karmic cycle is manifested), the soul plane (where we go following death on each of the lower 5 planes to select our next life or prepare for ascension) and finally the higher planes (attained only upon ascension).

Each of these dimensions has its own characteristic frequency vibrational rate. This rate increases in quality and intensity as we rise from the physical (lowest) plane to the God (highest) plane.

We possess a body of sorts on the lower 6 planes only. Matter is densest on the physical plane, and decreases in density as we rise up the spiritual ladder. Each dimension has certain learning centers where the soul may access its Akashic records and be advised by Masters and Guides. These institutions are referred to as Temples of Wisdom.

---

[1] B. Goldberg, "Past Lives-Future Lives" (New York: Ballantine, 1988).

The Lower Five Planes

The Earth Plane

The physical or Earth plane is the world we come to know in our present lives. Easterners refer to this dimension as the realm of illusion (maya), energy, matter, space and time. Although we are afforded an ideal environment here to work out much of our karma, we can also add to our karmic debts by our thoughts and actions. There are reportedly Temples of Wisdom located in certain Tibetan monasteries and in Peru. Thunder is the sound associated with the physical plane.

The Astral Plane

Spiritualists referred to the astral plane as Summerland. All phenomena we term psychic originate here. This includes telepathy, clairvoyance, poltergeists, telekinesis and so on. We divide the astral dimension into a lower and upper component. Souls who die and lead dysfunctional or negative lives end up in the lower astral plane. Demonic entities also reside here, which is why many people describe this dimension as hell. The Tibetans call this component of the astral plane bardo, while purgatory is the term used by Christians.

The upper astral plane is inhabited by more empowered souls who crossed into spirit from the physical plane. This dimension is shaped by the principles of form and imagination. On either level of the astral plane your emotions and thoughts create your reality.

We can compare these two aspects of the astral plane as follows:

Lower Astral Plane	Upper Astral Plane
Feelings of confusion and bewilderment	Feeling alert, secure, peaceful and happy
Misty or foggy environment.	Earthlike and beautiful environment with human inhabitants
The presence of bizarre and evil inhabitants	The presence of human inhabitants
Telepathic clairvoyant and precognitive experiences	Telepathic, clairvoyant and precognitive experiences
No possible spiritual growth or connection with your Higher Self	Connection with your Higher Self and unlimited Spiritual growth potential

Why Is There a Lower Astral Plane?

Do we really need the presence of a lower astral plane? There is no possibility of growth here due to indifference, prejudice and fear. The ancient Hermetic expression, "When the student is ready, the teacher will appear" is one explanation. It is only when lower astral plane souls specifically request guidance from their Higher Self and/or guides and enter the white light will they ascend to the higher astral plane, and eventually end up on the soul plane.

Other factors that help explain this are:

• Many souls feel comfortable being surrounded by the negativity of this lower astral plane. Their life on Earth often was quite dysfunctional, and they become conditioned to an environment of cynicism, depression and evil acts. In addition, from this dimension souls can observe their loved ones from their physical plane their physical plane life. The inability to break this astral form life. The inability to break this astral form of co-dependency keeps them stuck on this dimension as earthbound spirits.

•   Another factor relates to the brainwashing we are all exposed to by religion. The lower astral plane is equivalent to the Purgatory of Christianity and the bardo state of the Tibetans. If souls feel they are a sinners and haven't earned the right to enter heaven or nirvana, they will remain right where they are and continue to suffer.

•   The pleasures of astral sex also keep some souls from moving on. Sex with low-level astral entities is not particularly spiritual, but it does feel good nonetheless. Sexaholics on the physical plane will tend to satisfy their immediate gratification desires by continually participating in astral sex. This clouds their judgment and makes them much less receptive to entering the Light.

If a soul had a particularly poor or frustrating sex life while in the physical body, this only adds to the incentive to make up for lost time now. An astral body does not engage in the typical games people play on Earth. Molding with an astral lover is easy, and sex is readily available.

We observe an immense size to all buildings on the astral plane. It is literally impossible to describe these structures. It must be remembered that the astral plane is much larger than our physical plane.

The Astral Plane contains a great museum, where all inventions originate. It is said that such great minds as Edison, Telsa, Da Vinci, the Wright Brothers, Alexander Graham Bell and other inventors obtained their ideas by traveling to this museum. This gives new meaning to the Hermetic expression, "as above, so below."

The roar of the sea is the sound characteristic of the astral plane.

The Causal Plane

Our Akashic records, or files representing all of our past, present, parallel and future lifetimes, are located on this dimension. Each karmic lesson we have learned and failed to achieve are duly noted in these files. We can chart our soul's spiritual evolution by viewing these Akashic files.

We can access these records from any other plane through the use of hypnosis, or by visiting a learning temple. This is how a psychic reads your past, present or future. They simply access your Akashic records. Later in this chapter I will present an exercise for you to practice that will train you to read your own Akashic files.

The Akashic records themselves have been described as tiny objects resembling electromagnetic computer cards that were removed from a storage apparatus. You have the option of reading them directly, or viewing a hologram displaying scenes depicting the entire range of your current life or a past or future incarnation. We associate the tinkling of bells with this dimension.

The Mental Plane

Philosophy, moral teachings, thought, ethics and intellectual functions characterize the mental plane. It is on this plane that the Masters of conventional religions (Buddha, Jesus, etc.) spent most of their time during the waking state on the Earth plane, during which time they possessed a physical body.

It is postulated that the God(s) of orthodox religion is/are located here. The astral voyagers of ancient times who traveled to this dimension and had any type of contact with mental plane beings would easily identify them as a God.

The soil on the mental plane is blue, giving a deep blue appearance to their highways. Homes here are built in the style of abstract geometric designs. The common attire is a white flowing cloak, giving a mental plane entity the appearance of an angel.

The sound associated with this dimension is that of running water, while the "Om" sound also originates here.

The Etheric Plane

Truth and beauty are the most significant lessons our soul learns on the etheric plane. This plane is the source of our subconscious and primitive thoughts. This dimension appears flat to the soul traveler because of its vast size. Brilliant white lights dominate the sky of this plane, and one hears the sound of buzzing bees here.

We can summarize the characteristics of the astral through etheric planes as follows:

• **Physical Nature**

All dimensions beyond the Earth plane are composed of higher vibrational energy. This level increases as we go from the astral to etheric plane, resulting in each world appearing as less physical than our realm. Time does exist to a degree on these planes, but it is not as significant as within our three dimensional universe. There are no real outer boundaries as we would like to depict.

All worlds seem to occupy the same areas of space throughout all of space, each able to function independently of the other worlds because they are each vibrating at a different rate of energy. An inner plane spoken of as being higher or lower than another simply refers to a difference in vibration, not separation by linear distance.

Most of the people, buildings and landscapes of these other planes appear Earthlike. Some of the dimensions and structural configurations do seem a bit distorted by our Earthly standards.

- **Physical Laws**
  There are no physical laws on these dimensions as we know on Earth. Gravity is nonexistent, as we can fly anywhere by merely thinking of a location. We appear to be weightless, but can walk on the ground if we choose. The buildings and other structures remain on the ground because our thoughts plant them there and are not subject to gravitational laws.

- **People**
  Most of the inhabitants on these planes appear Earthlike in every way. There are people of different races, ethnic background and of varied ages. Only a small percentage of these souls resemble alienlike creatures or cartoon characters. The lower astral plane is the home of elements from occultist literature.

- **Language**
  English is spoken, if that is your native language on the physical plane. Whatever language you are comfortable with will be spoken on these other planes. Most communication is by telepathy.

You might be wondering how you can distinguish which plane you are on. There are three methods to distinguish your dimensional location:

1. Your Masters and Guides or Higher Self can inform you of which plane you are currently on.
2. The landmarks and uniqueness previously described can assist in your identification of which dimension is available to your consciousness.
3. Each plane has a characteristic sound associated with it. For example, if you heard the roar of the sea, this would indicate the Astral Plane. The tinkling of bells tells you that the

Causal Plane is your current location and so on. Voyagers from another plane, who do not have an Earth life, would hear the sound of thunder as they enter the Physical Plane.

Another consideration to understand about these other dimensions is that each plane has its own bureaucracy of Masters and Guides that oversees its operation. These perfect beings are in charge of creativity, space, time, and other physical workings of the lower universes, and function to prevent negative forces from upsetting the balance on this dimension.

The Soul Plane

After crossing into spirit on any of the lower five planes, our soul ends up eventually on the Soul Plane. On this dimension we have complete access to our Masters and Guides and Higher Self. These perfect entities help us in selecting a future lifetime. We may also access our Akashic records here.

Free will is still the rule here, so we may accept or reject the recommendations of our spiritual advisors. Your karma and spiritual growth are your responsibility alone. Your memories of these experiences will improve as the level of spiritual evolution increases. The learning center on this plane is the Temple of the Param Akshar. A single note of a flute is the sound heard often on this dimension.

An Exercise to Access the Akashic Records

The experience of drawing upon the Akashic records often presents itself to your waking awareness in visual form accompanied by the more essential sounds. Occasionally though it will be entirely auditory, as though someone were standing close behind you telling you what has taken place or will occur in the future. The information you receive is actually vibratory in nature, somewhat like the impressions on a magnetic tape. The images you see or hear are all from your own mind and have been stirred into activity by the Akashic

vibrations you have contacted. This accounts to some degree
for the variations in the forecast of the same event by two
different people. Each makes the same vibratory contact but
realizes it according to the experiences in his own image
storehouse.

With this background, try the following exercise:

1.   Use any of the previous self-hypnosis or other exercises
        to relax and apply white light protection. Lie down or
        sit in an easy chair and when you are relaxed turn your
        attention inward and center it on the area of the third
        eye. See it glow with a golden white radiance and feel
        it pulsate with energy. As you do this, your realization
        of the sounds, colors and temperature in the room
        around you should gradually fade and as they do so the
        subtle psychic stirrings will become more noticeable.

2.   At first, this may be only an impression of inner light or
        of brilliantly illuminated geometrical figures, or of stars
        shooting by in ordered procession, or some other visual
        appearance that will probably be meaningless. Or your
        first impression may be of sound, as I have previously
        described.

3.   Focus your mind, not on the Akashic records
        themselves, but on a specific historical event for your
        initial trials. For example, I suggest first you read up on
        the discovery of radium by Madame Curie or the signing
        of the Declaration of Independence in 1776.

4.   Your next step is to go to that historical event and ask
        yourself, "What happened that afternoon?" If you have
        properly prepared yourself, you will find yourself
        drifting into a scenariolike dream.

In the earlier stages of your development you will not get
clearly defined contacts that you can recognize as such, so don't
expect them. Accept the dreamlike sequence that passes before

your consciousness as you sit in reverie. Remember what you observe and write it down as soon as possible thereafter.

5.   During these practice sessions you should "feel" this connection between your waking consciousness and the Akasha. When this has been accomplished and you can recall an incident from the past as simply as you can look up an account in the encyclopedia, you are then ready to move on to the next step.

6.   The next step is to repeat the previous steps, omitting the preparation phase consisting of reading about the historical event beforehand.

7.   Next, check your data with specialty books written about that event in detail, not merely an encyclopedia summary.

8.   After successful completion of this step, move on to your own future. Begin with a short range, say one week to a month. Log all your observations into a journal and occasionally verify the accuracy of your prophecies.

9.   With a proven track record you are now ready to venture much farther ahead in time in your current life. Try five years, ten years, fifty years and so on.

10.   You may move several hundred years into the future and explore future lives. My books *Past Lives—Future Lives and Soul Healing* describe nearly 20 such cases as far forward as the thirty-eighth century!

11.   Last, tap into the general Akasha and allow your consciousness to tune into future world events, inventions, lifestyle changes and so on.

Remember, the key to successful application of these techniques is proper motivation and attitude and practice. Once you have developed a working connection between your Higher Self, it is not too difficult to contact the Akasha. Since the information in these records encompasses every event since this world began and many events still to come, your first attempts may result in confusion.

For instance, you may receive data from events 75,000 years ago, 150 years back, 10 years in the future and 500 years hence, all in rapid succession. This often results in a haphazard overlapping and indistinguishable mess. By directing your mind with specific goals, you can significantly reduce this effect.

In your own life you most likely have inadvertently received data from the Akasha. Often the scene or event observed is not recognized for what it is and if recalled at all is classified as a trick of the memory or imagination. Even when the vision is so clear that the perceiver is impressed, there is usually no clue as to when in the future it may occur. A conscientious application of this exercise will sharpen your psychic abilities and result in far more accuracy and spiritual empowerment.

Time Travel on the Other Planes

Once we leave the physical plane, the laws of the universe we have come to know cease to exist. Now our perspective is the space-time continuum, where all time is simultaneous. This is like entering the eye of a hurricane.

When we want to move to the past or future, as we would term it, all that is required is a focus of our attention on that time period and we will be transported there on these other dimensions. The problem with perceiving a specific date is one of focus and requires practice.

Many methods have been devised to time travel on these other planes. Some techniques applied are to imagine a clock face with its hands rapidly turning forward or backward. This technique is useful for shorter time-travel journeys. For longer trips, images of a calendar with pages being torn off or flipping back or forward in time seem to give excellent results.

Reports from my patients, along with my own personal voyages, bring to the surface certain limitations to dimensional time travel. First, you only the option only of going to certain time locations.   If the knowledge of this time era would significantly interfere with your spiritual growth or that of others, you will not be allowed access to this data.   There are certain areas of "forbidden knowledge" that apply. I explain this concept more fully in my book, *Astral Voyages.*[2]

Some time travelers may be easily able to obtain a scene three days in the future, but find it impossible to venture forward by 12 hours. These "windows in time" appear more difficult to master the farther we attempt to traverse time. An example of this principle is the fact that you may not have difficulty in moving to an event two years hence, but scenes five years in the future may be out of your reach. However, moving ahead 250 years from now may require little effort.

Many theories have been proposed to explain this phenomena. They range from the forbidden knowledge hypothesis I previously cited to the fact that our reality intersects the realities of other time zones (and parallel universes) at continuously changing locations. I present a rigorous discussion of this quantum physics paradigm in my book *Soul Healing.*

The earth time that elapses when you travel into the past or future on these other dimensions is quite inconsistent with our physical plane concept of time. For instance, only a few minutes may have elapsed on the physical plane during a sojourn to the twenty-fifth century encompassing a month or more.

The opposite occurs as you travel back in time.   A movement back in time to the Middle Ages that required only a few seconds of real time may actually have involved several minutes on the physical plane.

Other observations concern color perception. The farther you travel back in time, the duller the colors appear. These colors may take the appearance of a black-on-white mono-

---

[2] B. Goldberg, "Astral Voyages," op cit.

chrome as you venture very far back in history. Moving into the future results in a sharpening of color perception. This becomes almost a psychedelic effect, as colors appear quite brilliant the farther ahead you go. This principle applies equally to the other senses of sound, touch, taste and feeling.

Taking Charge of Your Life by Time Travel

We can apply these time-travel concepts to effect a very special type of psychic empowerment by influencing our own destiny. You may preview your own future on the physical plane and effect changes that result in different outcomes to circumstances you are facing now. A very practical application of this technique is to use this information to make or change decisions relevant to your life at this time. You can also influence the actions of others.

Suppose you had an important job interview and wanted to make a good impression on the interviewer beforehand. By using an out-of-body approach you could meet with the individual on the astral plane and establish a friendship with that person during this interdimensional voyage.

Since the Hermetic expression "like attracts like" has been passed down from antiquity, we know that the behavior you exhibit and attitude you manifest is critical to your spiritual growth. If you act in a negative fashion, you will attract negativity into your life. The reverse is also true. This principle is even more exaggerated on the astral plane, where very thought and desire materialize instantly.

Here are some simple principles of ethics that will keep you from getting into astral trouble:

• Keep your motives pure. If your "heart of hearts" is stimulated by greed, vengeance, insecurity or any other negative reason, think twice about acting on this impulse. "What goes around comes around" is applicable here. You may also look upon this as a "do unto others" approach.

• The universe presents lessons to allow us to learn. Do not feel that you are being punished when things don't go as you would like. Furthermore, it is not your purpose to play God and try to harm others or manipulate them. Part of our spiritual growth is to overcome the tendency to retaliate against the actions of others.

• Material benefits. There is nothing wrong with accumulating wealth and other physical plane rewards as a result of your astral voyaging. As long as you don't try to harm anyone or violate any universal law, your attempts at "karmic capitalism" will be successful and add to your growth in general.

Motivation and actions are what count the most in exercising these psychic empowerment techniques. You can use these methods to improve your life in many categories. Some of these include:

• Finding a soulmate
• Establishing peace of mind
• Developing friendships
• Improving your health
• Money
• A better job
• Psychic development

These goals may sound like pure materialism, but think again. Anything you can do to better your life without harming others allows you to be independent, happy and empowered. This also results in the reduction of fears, a necessary step to achieve ascension status.

I am most definitely not advocating ruthless or selfish behavior. These principles were not designed for you to control others. Through the application of spiritual ethics, discipline, goal orientation and a willingness to work within the parameters of the universe's design, you can control your own future and empower yourself, while becoming familiar with the fascinating universe of the other planes.

The Seven Higher Planes

The soul plane is the farthest we can travel until we have perfected the energy of our consciousness. Ascension to the higher planes on our way to God is our reward for achieving perfection. This is now possible because the soul's frequency vibrational rate is high enough to enter the seventh plane. When a further increase in its frequency vibrational rate occurs, it moves to the eighth plane and so on until it finally reaches the 13th or God plane. Another option for our perfect soul is to remain as a Master or Guide and assist other less-evolved souls to reach their state of ascension or perfection.

Since this paradigm represents hell as the lower astral plane, we can see that our conception of eternal damnation is all wrong. You can move from the lower astral plane into the upper astral and eventually reside on the soul plane. There is no eternal hell. However, there is a heaven. Spiritual growth is necessary at all levels of this system. This growth is achieved by practice and living a spiritual incarnation.

Describing the higher planes is always difficult, since the data is obtained through second-hand sources. We cannot enter these planes until we are perfect. No one on the Earth plane is perfect, so this information must be relayed by way of our Higher Self and spirit guides.

One method to receive this data is to do what I refer to as a soul plane ascension. This voyage guides you to this soul plane where you may receive depictions of the higher plane. A script for this technique is presented in Chapter 13.

The higher planes are hard to describe. These worlds lack any form of negativity. There is a freedom from what we call cause and effect, or causality. The reason for this is that we can only have an effect in relation to a finite mode of being. There is no such state on the higher plane, merely a nowness, isness and hereness.

God's energy is abundant throughout the higher planes. It is the omnipresence of God that denotes His identity and represents the isness. Nowness describes the reality of God being in the present time. Nowness may also be thought of as a stillness of motion, from which we will have the opportunity to live forever in this moment.

Space is the meaning of hereness. God is always here and the horizon that it encompasses is the hereness of God. In order to ascend we must empty our mind of everything (nothingness) and look within our consciousness to our Higher Self. Our Higher Self can venture into the higher planes because it is perfect. It stays with us on the soul planes and lower five planes to function as our guide.

Eternity, as represented by the higher planes, has neither time nor space as we know it. We really should not think of ascension as traveling to God. We are already a part of God. There is no space to travel to. When we become aware, know and look, we realize that we already occupy all, and this is our first step toward ascension.

The spirit that we and all inhabitants of the various planes possess emanates from God. This spirit allows the worlds to exist and function properly. We can think of God as a huge energy vortex, both transmitting energy in the form of spirit and bringing this energy back to Him. All life is both touched by it and sustained as a result of the interaction. This ocean of love is the basis of the universe.

The 13th or nameless plane is the home of the one true God energy. This is the region of the universe of truth or ultimate reality. This dimension is so beautiful and full of light that we cannot comprehend it from our position on the Earth plane.

The difference between the higher planes and lower planes is one of the frequency vibrational rate of our soul's energy.

It is your thoughts (motives) and actions that determine

your frequency vibrational rate. This level of consciousness or spiritual growth is completely within your own control. The more you grow spiritually the higher this rate. To reach the higher planes your frequency vibrational rate must be so high and pure that it can't even support a body of any kind. The soul plane is the last dimension in which we occupy any form of body.

We find that neither cause and effect nor logic per se exists in the higher planes. To have cause and effect we must create the illusion of succession. A change in seasons, birth and death and so on illustrate this concept. The higher planes are devoid of this mechanism.

Since all souls on the higher planes are perfect, there are no victims or perpetrators of evil acts. Logic is not needed, since there is no possibility of harming another. Each inhabitant of the higher planes formulates his or her own rules and lives by them.

The following chart illustrates this plane concept:

God or Nameless Plane (Plane 13)		
Seven Higher Planes	Plane 12	
	Plane 11	
	Plane 10	
	Plane 9	
	Plane 8	
	Plane 7	
Soul Plane (Plane 6)		
Karmic Cycle (Lower Five Planes)	Etheric Plane 5	Subconscious
	Mental Plane 4	Mind
	Causal Plane 3	Akashic Records
	Astral Plane 2	Emotions
	Earth Plane 1	You Are Here

Figure 2 – The Plane Concept

The relationship of these planes to one another is not one on top of the other. Neither is this paradigm one of farther out or beyond a certain dimension. These planes simply exist. They may occupy the same space at the same time, as do temperance, sound and light coexist. Our consciousness is the result of the interaction of these planes with our Higher Self and filtered down to our subconscious mind.

Earlier I described the various sounds and other characteristics of the lower planes. Figure 3 shows this relationship to all 13 planes.

The Creative Energy Sound

The way in which our soul is transported to these various dimensions is by a creative energy sound wave. This has been called Nada Brahma by the Buddhists, Vadon by the Sufis, Shabda Dun of the Hindus and Bani.

Name of Plane	Sound	Description
13. God of nameless Plane		The true Heaven or Nirvana
12.	Indescribable orchestra-like music is heard continually representing the sounds of the universe	The details of these planes can only be ascertained when you have ascended. There is no time, space or cause and effect here. Souls occupying Eternity do not possess a body of any kind. They are all perfect energy
11.		
10.		
9.		
8.		
7.		
6. Soul Plane	Single note of a flute	This is where souls go following death on the lower 5 planes to choose their next life. Beyond this plane there is no body of any type. Self-realization and ascension occurs here

5. Etheric (Intuition)	Buzzing of bees	The source of the Subconscious
4. Mental (Mind)	Running water	The source of moral ethics and philosophy. The home of the God of most orthodox religions
3. Casual (Memory)	Tinkle of bells	Akashic records are kept here
2. Astral (Emotion)	Roar of the sea	The source of emotions and all psychic phenomena.
1. Physical (5 Senses)	Thunder	Illusion of reality; the plane of space, time, matter and energy

Figure 3. The Sounds and Descriptions of the 13 Planes

The reception and perception of these sound waves is the responsibility of our chakras. These chakras are energy centers located within and above our astral body. I describe these chakras in greater detail in Chapter 6.

The metaphysical literature suggests that this sound is produced by the humming of atoms as they flow out from God's center into the worlds below via the great sound wave, which touches all things (world-soul). This sound expands through our seven major chakras.

The creative sound functions to awaken the inner consciousness and connection with God. The bells and gongs of religious services, Gregorian chants, mantras used by the Orientals, the horns blown by the yogis, and the double flute of the Sufi dervishes are other examples of this principle.

Through the use of this great sound wave our consciousness may transcend the physical body. The sounds associated with the various lower planes are commonly heard in the right ear just prior to an out-of-body experience. We will present exercises in Chapter 13 to train you to have such experiences.

The only thing that can limit your spiritual growth is fear and your mind's desire. Your consciousness will be expanded and you will be presented with knowledge that facilitates your awareness, knowledge and mastery of the other dimensions in which all that constitutes the true universe exists when you practice the techniques presented in this book. In addition to understanding your karmic purpose, you will make significant progress toward your own ascension.

Chapter 6

Yogic Exercises for Ascension

*B*efore I present various yogic exercises designed to train the student for ascension, the ultimate goal from a yogic point of view needs to be discussed. The eighth and final stage of hatha yoga is samadhi, or bliss. This is a merging with one's superconscious mind.

This samadhi state transcends the merely mental condition of intellectual contemplation, and goes on to the state of ecstasy. The attainment of such a condition for the ordinary person is difficult. A mystic union of the individual soul with the Universal Soul is represented by the God Shiva and Goddess Shakti in Indian theology. All normal mental processes are suspended; the traffic of the senses is brought to a standstill; the ego is extinguished. All things become one; differences vanish and the oneness of the self and the Infinite is apprehended in the highest dimensions. This is ascension.[1]

Some have described this state as the voice of the inner silence. This is where no sound dwells but where sound emanates. A pinpoint of silence is accompanied by a vision of

---

[1] M. Eliade, "Yoga, Immortality and Freedom" (Princeton, N.J.: Princeton University Press, 1970).

light that passes from a bright glow to a heaven full of brilliant dots, like stars; then to geometrical radiances and colored shapes. All this is experienced in the sixth chakra, or third-eye region of our astral body. Following this a sudden whiteness becomes an awareness of the supreme Light of God.

The Chakras

I have alluded to the chakras before. It is only through meditation or other alpha techniques that we can perceive these energy centers. A chakra represents the actual juncture between our physical and astral bodies. We have hundreds of such intersections, but only seven major chakras.

These major chakras are arranged along a shaft of the astral body that is believed to pass through the human frame from the base of the spine to the top of the head. This shaft, called the Rod of Brahma, is located within the spinal column. The Rod of Brahma is also known as the gateway of ascent.

Each chakra is compared to an inverted flower bud pointing downward; as it is pierced through the practice of ascension techniques, it folds down upon itself, closes into a tight ball and then blossoms out, its petals unfurled and facing upward.

The first major chakra is at the base of the spine, near the tail bone (called the muladhara); the next is in the region of the sex organs; the third in the region of the solar plexus; the fourth at the level of the heart; the fifth at the base of the throat; the sixth behind the meeting-point of the eyebrows; and the seventh just above the crown of the head called the sahasrara). Figure 4 shows the location of these chakras with our physical body.

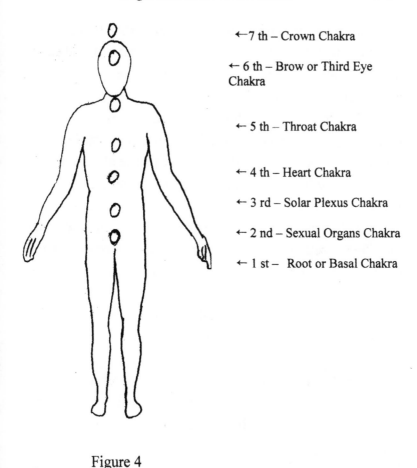

← 7 th – Crown Chakra

← 6 th – Brow or Third Eye Chakra

← 5 th – Throat Chakra

← 4 th – Heart Chakra

← 3 rd – Solar Plexus Chakra

← 2 nd – Sexual Organs Chakra

← 1 st – Root or Basal Chakra

Figure 4

The opening of the basal chakra confers regenerative power; the solar plexus gives control over the internal processes; the heart plexus controls the subtle winds; the throat chakra the etheric elements; the eye chakra rules elemental beings; and the sahasrara brings ultimate understanding of Nature's mysteries.

Ascension follows a series of disciplines in yogic techniques. This purification of the soul may result from the combination of bodily postures (asanas), hand gestures (mudra), mystic syllables (mantra), breath control (pranayama), eye focusing (trataka), symbolic diagrams (yantra), and super-concentration (dharana). In this chapter we will focus on asanas and breath control.

When the yoga practitioner is nearing an ascension state, certain unusual sounds will be heard within the consciousness, not externally, of the individual. The sequence of these sounds begins with a high shrill, like the chirping of crickets. This shrill sound begins to change. It is lowered in pitch and becomes like the buzzing of a bee, then a dull drone, the sound of a flute, a bell, a deeper boom, and then the roar of a distant ocean. If you refer to figure 3 in chapter 5, you will note that some of these sounds are characteristic of the other planes.

Before we begin with breath control techniques, try this simple neck roll exercise to relax your body.

1. Stand erect. Allow your head to drop forward as far as it will go so that your chin comes down onto your chest. Relax all the muscles and let your head hang loosely.

2. Then slowly move your head to the right until it is now hanging loosely over your right shoulder. Do not look to the right but continue to face directly ahead. Sometimes it helps to perform this before a mirror at first until you get accustomed to it.

3. Next roll your head toward the rear until it hangs in a relaxed manner as far back as your neck will allow while your gaze is (or should be) toward the ceiling.

4. Then roll your head toward the left shoulder and make sure you are once again facing forward.

5.   Finish the circle by bringing the head once again to the original position, hanging relaxed down toward your chest.

6.   This exercise should be performed as one complete motion but quite slowly. A count of 12 should be about right for the complete revolution. Make three revolutions.

7.   Repeat the same process in the opposite direction, starting by dropping the head down forward on the chest, then to the left shoulder, then to the back, then to the right shoulder and finish with the head hanging loosely down toward the front.

During this exercise your breathing should be entirely relaxed and normal. No attempt should be made to take especially deep breaths or to hold the breath in or out at any time.

Breath Control

The fourth stage of hatha yoga is concerned with pranayama, or breath control, which takes into account a number of factors. First comes the simple technique of inhalation, retention and exhalation, for which a ratio has to be established. A common ratio adopted is 3-2-3: three units for drawing the breath in, two for retaining it and three for expelling it. The unit, known as the matra, may be one second or other fraction of a minute, but is usually calculated by the time it takes to stroke the knee with a circular motion three times and then snap the finger and thumb once.

The breathing is then diffused into two streams of subtle

breath (prana): an upward moving breath from below, and a downward moving breath, both breaths being directed toward the diaphragm to be collected there as if charging a battery.

Sometimes another item is added to the rhythm of inhalation, retention and exhalation, namely, retention of breath after exhalation, and we then have to add a fourth element to our ratio, thus getting 3-2-3-2, or whatever the ratio may be.

Next, try this yogic breathing method known as the Bellows Breath:

> Sit upright in a comfortable chair and breathe in deeply through your nostrils so they become flared. Repeat this several times at the frequency of once per second. In the beginning limit yourself to four deep breaths to prevent dizziness. With conditioning you should reach the level of ten breaths.

The air breathed in is not in itself the essential element utilized by the yogi. The air we breathe only serves as the conductor for this subtle force. This energy is called prana, and pranayama teaches the method of absorbing it. Pranayama is the controlled means by which the invisible energy of the cosmos is channeled to act directly on the physical system.

Here is another breathing exercise to assist you in developing your pranayama technique:

1.   Stand erect, raise your arms simultaneously up from your sides until they are outstretched and parallel to the ground. As you do this take a deep breath and hold it.
2.   While holding the breath bring your arms down in front

of you so that they form an X with your hands pointing at the ground. As you do this imagine that you are pulling down great weights. This will give a firm tone to the muscles of your arms, shoulders and back.

3.   Hold the arms in the crossed downward position for the count of eight and continue to hold your breath as well. As you do this imagine your breath going to the base of the spine in the form of energy.

4.   After the count of eight, exhale, relax your arms, letting them drop to your sides as you resume your original erect posture.

Perform this exercise three times at first, but after three weeks increase it to seven times each exercise period.

This is a more advanced breathing technique:

1.   Sit in a straight-back chair with both feet flat on the floor and your spine held in an erect position.

2.   Breathe in slowly through the left nostril. If necessary, hold the right nostril closed by pressing it with your finger. After a little practice you will find that you will be able to direct the flow of your breath into the proper nostril without blocking off the other.

As you breath in through the left nostril send your breath from the throat down the left side of your spine to its base. Do this to the count of four.

3.   Now hold your breath to the count of ten, and as you do, feel it energizing the center at the base of your spine.

4.   Now cover your left nostril and allow your breath to escape slowly through the right nostril to the count of eight. As you do this visualize the breath leaving the

base of the spine, traveling up its right side and out the right nostril.

5.   Now repeat the process but start this time by covering the left nostril and inhaling for the count of four through the right nostril. As you do this feel the breath going from the throat down the right side of your spine to its base.

6.   Hold your breath at the base of the spine for the count of ten and then permit it to escape up the left side of your spine and out the left nostril while you count to eight.

I suggest you practice this technique once daily for the first three weeks. You may then gradually increase this to a maximum of three repetitions during each exercise period. In addition to muscle building and toning, the exercises, particularly numbers 4 and 5, are designed to stimulate the first chakra at the base of the spine and start its energy flowing upward to the brain.

Yogis are able to suspend their breathing to an abnormal extent; show different pulse rates at will on the right and left wrists; lower the respiratory rate until it is barely perceptible; become totally immunized to the effects of heat and cold; remain in trance for days at a time; go without food and water for several weeks; exert an almost supernatural control over wild animals.

Ascension is the ultimate goal of yoga. The body is the physical instrument through which these goals are achieved, and its demands must therefore be disciplined and controlled before samadhi, "final bliss," can be attained. Yogic scripture stresses incorporating these breathing exercises with other yogic practices and under the guidance of a teacher or guru.

Yogic Asanas

Before I present advanced asanas designed to prepare you for ascension, basic postures are recommended to relax your body and condition you for more complicated asanas or postures. One definition of relaxation is a complete resignation of the body to the power of gravity, surrender of the mind to nature, and the whole body energy being transferred to a deep, dynamic breathing.

Complete relaxation of the voluntary muscles at once transfers energy to involuntary parts so that, strictly speaking, there can be no such thing as relaxation except in the voluntary muscles and brain. This transfer of energy by voluntary action and involuntary reaction produces the necessary equilibrium for the renewal of strength and mental relaxation. When you regularly practice these basic asanas, you will notice a new keenness of mind and an ability to utilize your nerve-energy to the utmost for whatever personal goals you may have set for yourself.

Three basic asanas for complete relaxation are the Firm Asana, Corpse Asana and Relaxed Asana.

Firm Asana

The Firm Asana is the most relaxing pose and is designed for improved sleep.

Lie down with your right arm under your head, using it as a pillow. By lying passively on the right side, you favor emptying of the stomach and make breathing movements easier.

Corpse Asana

The purpose of the Corpse Asana is to eliminate fatigue and quiet the mind.

1. Lie face up with your feet extended. Remain motionless with a sense or feeling of sinking down like a corpse.
2. Gradually relax every muscle of the body by concentrating on each individually, from the tip of the toe to the end of the skull.
3. Do the best you can to detach yourself from any thoughts concerning your body.
4. Stay in this pose until you feel recharged.

If this pose is kept for more than ten minutes, the deepened respiration and lowered circulation in the brain will probably bring about a tendency to sleep.

Relaxed Asana

1. Lie down with your head on your folded arms, as if on a pillow, and concentrate as in the Firm Asana.
2. Relax all your muscles systematically. Stretch your hands and legs out fully, and permit the power of gravity to take over the weight of your body as you relax every voluntary muscle.

Stretching Asanas

Once you have achieved a relaxed state, you are now ready for some basic stretching poses. These asanas were designed to exercise the spine, restore tonicity in the spinal muscles and open up our nerve channels for more efficient functioning.

Snake Asana

1. Lie on your stomach, with your legs stretched and toes pointed outward. Keep your arms at your sides, with palms down, and your forehead on the floor. Then, slowly raise your head and neck upward and backward.

2. When your head and neck are slightly raised, plant your hands on both sides of the abdomen. Inhale, and gradually raise your thorax and the upper part of your abdomen by increasing the angle between your hands and rising shoulders. From the navel downward, your body should remain fixed to the ground. Only the upper portion of your body should be raised.

3. Work toward this pose gradually, avoiding muscular strain or "jerkiness" in your efforts to raise the upper part of your body. As you practice this pose, you will feel the pressure on your spinal column gradually working down the vertebrae until you feel a deep pressure at the coccyx.

4. Having achieved the correct pose, exhale and return to the starting position. Lower yourself slowly.

After the pose has been mastered, follow this procedure: (1) Raise thorax and inhale for three seconds; (2) maintain pose, retaining your breath for six seconds; (3) return to starting position, while exhaling for three seconds; (4) repeat five times in a minute.

Plough Asana

The Plough Asana is designed to be practiced when you are fully rested.

1. Lie on the floor with your face upward and arms resting at your sides, palms downward. Then raise your legs together, slowing inhaling until your legs are brought at a right angle to the body.

2. While exhaling slowly, raise your hips and lower your legs beyond your head. Keep your legs together and straight. As you become practiced in this posture, stretch your toes farther and farther beyond your head.

To condition your legs for this posture, try these exercises: (1) Raise legs to a right angle with body and inhale for two seconds; (2) lower legs beyond head and exhale for two seconds; (3) maintain pose for four seconds while suspending breath; (4) return to starting position, while inhaling slowly for two seconds.

Camel Asana

The Camel Asana is the most advanced asana of these basic postures.

1. Kneel and while supporting your body on your toes gradually lean backward, after fixing your arms behind you, with your palms to the ground, fingers pointed

outward and thumbs toward your toes.
2. Keeping your arms straight, slowly lift your hips while inhaling. The body-lift should take three seconds with inhalation; retention, six seconds; return to kneeling position while exhaling, three seconds.
3. Now push your body above the waist slowly outward and upward, throwing your neck downward. As you come into this posture, you should feel the pressure traveling upward toward your shoulders and neck, finally reaching your neck and facial muscles.

Advanced Yogic Asanas

In their highest form, yogic asanas, or poses, are practiced in combination with breathing techniques, with the recitation of mantras, with mudras, and with mandalas, or mystic diagrams. In such an asana the whole body becomes a plastic mold into which etheric forces are drawn down and poured forth from the other planes, filling the mold represented by the asana and imbuing it with the desired power.

Prayer Asana

This asana is used for standing prayer. By coordinating skeletal muscles and correcting postural defects, it permits a normal standing posture.

1. While standing, hold your body as tall as possible without actually rising on your toes. Keep your heels together, placing all your weight upon the balls of your feet. Throw your head and chest up, shoulder blades flat. The abdominal muscles should be deflated

at their lower part, but not drawn inward, and fuller just below the ribs, while the pelvis should be tilted at such an angle as to prevent any exaggeration of the lumbar curve.

2.   Your knees must be straight but not stiff, with legs together touching at the knees. Fold your hands over the sternum, avoid tension. Relax your mind and fix your eyes on any pleasing object before you.

3.   In this position, the thorax is full and round; the diaphragm is high; the abdomen at its greatest length. The stomach and intestinal viscera are held in proper place and the pelvic organs are relieved of pressures from above. There is a partial relaxation of the larger muscles and relief from tension.

4.   Maintain this position for about one minute, breathing normally. Keep your mind free and observe complete silence. Turn slowly to either side, parallel to a wall or post, and notice whether you sway. Swaying is an indication of nervous disturbance which must be overcome.

It is best to practice this asana in front of a mirror, where you can observe any swaying. Keep your eyes half closed during your practice time, and focus your concentration on your body above the waist. Stand immobile as a statue, and as soon as you have a tendency to sway, check it by conscious effort. After the first few weeks, try to sustain this motionless pose for two to three minutes, always breathing normally. This pose is best practiced in the morning, and should be followed daily until complete control has been achieved. Afterward, it may be practiced once weekly.

Stick Asana

This pose developed during the nineteenth century is purported to increase the height of the student. One thing we do know about this asana is that it creates a state of complete relaxation if practiced properly.

1.   Lie on your back on a comfortable mat or carpet, with your legs and arms fully extended. With body supine, arms and legs outstretched, inhale for three seconds.
2.   While your body is outstretched, hold your breath for three seconds.
3.   Return to the starting position; exhale for three seconds.

Repeat the entire exercise five times in one minute.

Any maximum stretching of the body should be attempted only while the breath is retained. Do not attempt to hold your breath for more than four or five seconds. According to yogic theory, stretching aids height, and its regular practice at least slows down, if not stops, the tendency to lose height as one ages.

One-leg Asana

This pose relaxes and exercises the muscles of both legs. When swaying is experienced during this exercise, the best corrective is to concentrate your mind on each of your movements. Become consciously aware of the most insignificant variations in steadiness, so that you will be able to secure control over all movement.

1.   Assume the Prayer Asana first. Bend down, lift one leg with your hand and bring it up to the thigh. Keep your balance on the other leg.

2.   After you have attained sufficient steadiness on one leg, adjust the raised leg by pressing the heel tightly against the opposite groin, with the sole of the foot against the opposite thigh.

3.   Maintain this pose for two minutes, and repeat using the other leg.

At first it may be necessary to use some support to maintain balance. Later you will be able to practice without support, maintaining this pose with your hands in the prayer posture.

Lotus Asana

The Lotus Asana is designed to improve the flexibility of the muscles attached to the pelvis and lower extremities. You should avoid the use of a bare floor. If the room in which you are practicing is not carpeted, provide yourself with a soft mat at least 6 x 3 feet, and spread a clean sheet over the area where you will sit or lie.

1.   Sit on the floor with your legs stretched out. Bend the right leg slowly and fold it upon itself. Using your hands, place the right heel at the root of the thigh so that its sole is turned upwards and your foot is stretched over the left groin.

2.   Similarly, bend the left leg and fold it upon itself with your hands, placing the left heel over the root of the right thigh. Your ankles should cross each other, while

your heel-ends touch closely. The left foot with its upturned sole should lie fully stretched over the right groin.

3.   Keep your knees pressed to the ground, feet tight against the thighs, and press your heels firmly against the upper front margin of the pubic bone slightly above the sex organs.

4.   To complete this pose, hold your body erect, with neck straight, chest thrown forward and abdomen drawn moderately inward. Fix your eyes on any object in front of you, then close them. Spread your left hand with its back touching both heels, palm upwards. Place your right hand over the left in the same manner.

This pose results in either extension, flexion or relaxation to almost all the important muscles, ligaments and tendons of the lower limbs. It also induces increased blood circulation in the abdominal and genital areas. The Lotus Asana also helps to tone the various nerve centers in the pelvic region. In this posture, it is important that the shoulders should not sag\ forward, crowding the chest, nor should the upper part of the body crowd down upon the stomach and the abdominal viscera.

Triangle Asana

The Triangle Asana will enable you to reach a state of physical suppleness and elasticity that will have a relaxing effect on your mental state. Because of the exceptionally straight and full-length adjustments of the bony structure of the spine, this pose will correct many of the ailments due to misplaced internal organs and poor body tonicity.

1.   Stand erect with your feet together and arms down at your sides. Slowly exhale while bending downward; keep your legs straight. Lower only the upper part of the body. Keep your legs perfectly straight and pressed backwards.

2.   Now touch your toes with the tips of your fingers, keeping your arms straight, with spine and neck horizontal, abdomen in, head thrown forward, and your eyes fixed on the tip of your nose. Maintain this pose and then return to the original position while inhaling.

3.   Your movements and timing should be as follows: (A) Touch toes and exhale for three seconds; (B) keep pose and hold breath for six seconds; (C) return to starting position and inhale for three seconds. Repeat five times in one minute without pausing.

Do not become discouraged if you fail to touch your toes on the first attempt. Try each day until you can hold the pose comfortably. Work into this pose gradually, avoiding attempts to force your body into it by jerks or sudden pulling of the muscles. Before working for other refinements of the pose, aim to touch your toes.

Here is a variation of the Triangle Asana.

1.   Stand with your feet 24 inches apart and, while inhaling, raise one arm and bend it laterally on the opposite side, sliding the other arm lengthwise. When

the complete lateral stretch is achieved, retain your breath and return to the original position. Repeat the lateral stretch on the other side.

2. Movements, breathing and timing should be as follows: (A) Bend sideward; inhale for three seconds; (B) keep pose and retain breath for six seconds; (C) return to normal position and exhale for three seconds. Repeat alternately, without pausing, ten times in two minutes.

Eagle Asana

1. Stand erect and lift one leg. Twist this same leg both near the hip joint and the knee. Then entwine one leg around the other. Adjust the twists very carefully without strain or muscle tension.

2. Lock the ankle with the toe of the other twisted leg and hold it there as a safety against possible accidental release. Do this while exhaling.

3. When you are balanced on one leg, make an effort to keep the body straight, and gradually increase the pressure of the toehold near the opposite ankle until the greatest possible twist is achieved.

4. Repeat steps 1 through 3 using the other leg.

At first, practice only the leg twist while retaining your breath. After the first week or so, when this becomes easier, try the arm and hand twists by entwining one arm around the other (alternating arms). Twist the hands from the wrists and press the palms against each other. Try to keep the pose for several seconds and, while inhaling, return to the original position.

Avoid straining while twisting with this pose. This asana should be practiced in gradual stages before you attempt to follow the full exercise.

Do not force yourself into this pose until your limbs have gained sufficient suppleness. Then you should follow this time-plan: (1) Twist your body and exhale for five seconds; (2) maintain this pose and retain your breath for ten seconds (or you may with normal, rhythmic breathing hold the pose for not more than two minutes); (3) return to starting position and inhale for five seconds.

Mountain Asana

The Mountain Asana is recommended for use in weight control and in correcting minor postural defects of the spinal cord.

1. Place yourself in the Lotus Asana, slowly raise your hands upward and above the head. Keep your palms pressed together.

2. Stretch upward as if to touch some object directly above your head. Keep your arms close to your ears, your head erect, your back straight, and pull your abdomen in.

3. Raise the upper part of your body to its maximum height while inhaling. Make sure your elbows and wrists are in a straight line.

During this exercise, keep your eyes fixed on some object before you and keep your mind at ease. Maintain its slightly stretched, upright position between breaths.

For maximum benefits, the movements and breathing should be in harmony. To attain this, try the following instructions: (1) In a sitting pose, raise arms and inhale for three seconds; (2) maintain pose and try to retain breath for six seconds; (3) return to starting position, exhale for three seconds. Repeat this pose five times to a minute without pausing.

You may be interested in trying four variations of this pose. The purpose of the variations is to provide additional stretching of all sets of muscles in the trunk. They also massage the internal organs just below the ribs and the abdominal muscles.

Here are the variations to the Mountain Asana: (1) Swaying forward; (2) leaning backward; (3) bending to the right; (4) bending to the left. These variations should be utilized during a six-second breathing pause. Instead of maintaining the perpendicular position while stretching, vary it by making the movements on the four sides and alternately. Gradually increase the retention of your breath to nine seconds, which will permit four movements to a minute. Here is a suggested daily regimen for these asanas:

Asanas	Time
1. Prayer Asana	1 Minute
2. Stick Asana	1 Minute
3. One-leg Asana	1 Minute
4. Lotus Asana	1 Minute
5. Triangle Asana	2 Minutes
6. Eagle Asana	2 Minutes
7. Mountain Asana	1 Minute
Total Time	9 Minutes

_____

*M*editation is a method of achieving calmness and concentration. Zen forms of meditation have as one of their goals a sudden illumination called satori. The ultimate purpose of this relaxation technique is to attain enlightenment and prepare our soul for ascension.

Meditation can take many forms: concentrating single-pointedly on an (internal) object, trying to understand some personal problem, generating a joyful love for all humanity, praying to an object of devotion, or communicating with our own Higher Self: Its ultimate aim is to awaken a very subtle level of consciousness and to use it to discover reality, directly and intuitively, resulting in a very special form of wisdom.

Many Westerners incorrectly assume meditation to be an escape from reality or a loss of consciousness. To practice this discipline properly you need a room where you will be undisturbed for from 15 to 30 minutes. Any position will work, as long as you are comfortable.

Having assumed a comfortable position, one should let the whole body relax. All the muscles must be loosened; all tension let go. Among the many aids used for inducing relaxation are rhythmic breathing; a gentle humming; a slight swaying of the torso while seated. Easiest of all, perhaps, is mentally going over the parts of the body in which tension is likely to occur, starting from the feet, then moving systematically up the body to the head.

The next procedure is to empty the mind of every possible distracting thought that blocks your connection with your Higher Self. Following this, a "one-pointedness" approach to focus concentration is enacted to train the mind to be firm and steady. This involves fixing the mind on a single object to the exclusion of all else.

Contemplation methods follow this concentration stage. This turning within to access one's Higher Self directs the consciousness inward. In this stage you must lose yourself from associating with the outside world. In yogic meditation the final stage is samadhi, or a state of oneness with one's superconscious mind.

Religions have presented their paradigms toward meditation illustrating a diverse menu. The ancient Chinese system is depicted in the Taoist teachings as Wu-Wei, or "nonstriving." There is no attempt to stir up consciousness using exhausting techniques, but through a natural quiet process of allowing the mind to quiet, resulting in a spontaneous revelation of the clear depths within.

Yogic meditation has a rather strict eight-stage process culminating in samadhi, as I have previously described the Zen Buddhist approach being a middle way between the stern practices of yoga and the methodlessness of Tao. Meditation here is largely a matter of keeping the mind quiet and still. We have discussed its goal of satori previously.

In Sufism there are several stages divided into two main groups: maqam, or man's effort, and hal, God's grace. It is said, "Maqam is earned; hal is gifted." Repetition of the name of God plays an important part in Sufi mysticism. The Sufi sits in solitude and without ceasing repeat the name of Allah, letting his mind dwell on the mercy and glory of God. He must persevere until his heart takes up the refrain, and mind, heart and soul are suffused with the idea of God in the fullness of His mercy and power.

When we consider these various theologies and the techniques they employ in their effort to attain enlightenment, beatitude or unity with the Absolute, it might be felt that the absence of a meditative regime in Christianity for the common man is a drawback to the contemplative life.

Christianity actually has quite a history with meditation. It was practiced by the early monks who dwelt in the desert regions of Egypt and Syria from the third century A.D. Their disciplines were at times so severe as to be scarcely credible today, and their experience with "temptation" by the Devil and elemental creatures are as vivid as any brought back by occultists from the astral planes. A system somewhat akin to yoga, with emphasis on breathing and concentration on the plexuses, was followed in Greece by various monk sects during the Middle Ages.

The Spiritual Exercises of St. Ignatius of Loyola outlines a stringent procedure in a contemplative process that has led many to spiritual exaltation. But the church does not normally advocate meditation for the layman, apart from the periods of retreat set aside for the purpose in the religious calendar, such as the days between Good Friday and Easter Sunday.

Some Christian denominations, among them several Quietist sects, practice various kinds of group meditation, where a number of persons gather together during service and sit in silence. In some cases a verse is read out from the Bible and the assembly simply bow their heads and meditate independently on its meaning. Something may or may not emerge from the group silence, but those who have attended such meetings have spoken of its beneficent influence in recharging the mind and spirit with dynamic power. The posture of meditation for the Christian is not face to face, implying equality with the Creator, but on bended knees with head bowed in humility.

These Christian approaches have as their goal a state of mind during which the soul is enriched by a more intense and unadulterated quality of love, intelligence, and strength than we have experienced before. The term for it is transcendence. Transcendence always involves the act of entering into an enriched and active state of mind; it is not just the escape from something unpleasant or mundane.

Visualization Helpful Hints

Many of the meditations in this chapter, as well as the hypnotic exercises in chapter 13, involve visual imagery. These guidelines and suggestions will assist you in maximizing your ability to visualize.

1. When you visualize an object imagine actually touching or holding it. Use your past experiences and memories to recreate its texture, color, shape and feel. The same suggestions apply to people.

2. Maintain an absolute conviction that the person or object you have created exists. The actions or other

characteristics associated with or caused by this person or thing is also to be assumed as happening or existing now.

1. Bring your other senses into play during a visualization. Hear the person or object, see it, touch it, and smell its fragrance.

2. Create a three-dimension hologram of this visual image. Have a sense as to its shape, position, volume and depth.

3. Give life to your imagery. Allow it to move, change and flow with your thoughts and feelings. Recreate any aspects of this visualization instantly if parts of it appear to fade.

4. Complete the details of these images. It doesn't matter how accurate your specific details are to the actual image itself. By keeping your focus on it, you are increasing its lifespan within your mind.

5. Refrain from censoring or editing a spontaneous image. Let it flow and develop to its own natural level of detail.

6. Do not allow abstract or symbolic images to confuse you or distract your focus. Simply let them arise and let your Higher Self direct you to your course of action.

A Basic Meditation System

Here is an overview of how a basic meditation progresses from start to finish:

1. Assume a meditative posture. You can use the Lotus Asana, or any other posture that suits you.

2.   Close your eyes and relax your body. Pay attention to what you can now hear. Focus on your breathing and breathe deeply for several breaths.

3.   Note any sensations you perceive and calm your emotional state.

4.   Quiet your thoughts. Narrow your cognitions to only one thing.

5.   Relax this effort to think of one thing only. Allow a few minutes to be in this state of mind.

6.   Return to normal consciousness.

The script I will now present is one of a breathing meditation. It is best to make a tape of this script in order to maximize its effect. My office carries a line of my tapes, including this one. You may contact my office for a complete list of these cassettes.

A Breathing Meditation

Focus all of your attention on your breath. Concentrate on the mechanics of breathing, not the thought of the breath. Note how it comes and goes. As the breath enters and leaves the nostrils, feel the expansion and contraction of the lungs.

Focus on the awareness of breathing. Remove all other thoughts and feelings from your awareness. Observe this natural life process. Do not try to change it. Merely be with it.

Let yourself receive the changing sensations that accompany this process. As you inhale and exhale, one breath at a time, let it happen by itself. If it is deep, let it be deep. If it is slow, let it be slow. If it is shallow, let it be shallow. If you sense the mind is interfering with this process, just focus on the inhalation and exhalation. Be one with your breath. Nothing else matters.

Observe the uniqueness of each breath. Observe, don't analyze. Note the changing sensations. Be one with your breath.

Ignore all other functions of the body. Remove all thoughts from your mind. You are the breath. Be one with your breath. You are now floating with the universe. As the wind carries a feather, you are being carried by your breath. Notice how the distracting thoughts fade. How they become meaningless. All that matters it that you breathe. You are your breath. Be one with your breath.

Let go of the body. Feel as if you have no body. You are weightless, as is your breath. You are floating in the universe. You are at peace with the universe. You are one with the universe. Notice how relaxed you are, now that you are free of . the confines of the body. You are totally one with the universe. There is nowhere to go. Nobody is expecting you. You have no schedule or deadline. You are free. Enjoy this moment for you are one with the universe.

Be quiet. Do not cough or make any movement or sound. Just be still and merge with the universe. You are consciousness. Let go of all fear and doubt. Let go of all thoughts. Do not try to control your being. Just be free and one with your consciousness.

You have no body. You have no limitations. You are one with your consciousness. You are one with the universe. Let each moment occur by itself. Observe it and enjoy these intervals of time. Do not resist this merging with your consciousness. You are now nothing but consciousness. You are the universe.

Now it is time to return to your body. Again, concentrate on your breath. Now note the other functions of your body. Slowly open up your eyes and do what you feel is important at this time.

A Meditation to Balance the Chakras

In chapter 6 I discussed the energy centers in our astral body known as the chakras. When these are out of alignment we are susceptible to disease,[1] and our spiritual growth is retarded.

Try this meditation to balance all seven of our major chakras:

1.   Relax, sit comfortably and take a deep breath. Hold this breath for a count of eight and exhale. Repeat this and hold this breath to a count of ten.

2.   Close your eyes and breathe normally. Visualize a band of energy rising up from the Earth and entering both your feet. Feel this energy vibrate and tingle as it moves past your knees and into your hip.

3.   Imagine a red color to this energy as it enters the first chakra in your sacrum. Take another deep breath as you perceive this color. Let this breath out slowly.

4.   Now inhale and imagine this energy turning orange as it enters the second chakra. Exhale slowly. As you inhale again see this color become yellow as it moves into the third chakra. Gently let your breath out.

---

[1] B. Goldberg, "Soul Healing" (St. Paul: Llewellyn, 1996).

5.   Inhale again and follow this energy as it enters the heart chakra where it turns green. Slowly exhale. Breathe in deeply and visualize the energy moving up o your throat chakra, as it now appears blue. Exhale slowly.

6.   Continue with your deep breathing as the energy enters into the third eye or sixth chakra and is seen as indigo.

7.   Now inhale again and see this energy leave from the top of your head or crown chakra, where it now appears as violet. Exhale gently and perceive this violet aura surrounding your entire body. Notice how this violet color changes to white and pulsates around your entire physical body creating a wonderful relaxing and protective feeling.

8.   Stay with this image and feeling for five minutes. Open up your eyes.

A Relaxation Meditation

1.   Sit in a comfortable chair, relax and close your eyes. Breathe deeply for 30 seconds.

2.   Let your arms rest loosely with the hands open, palms up, on the thighs. The elbows should be relaxed. Clench your fists tightly then let them slowly unclench. Remember this feeling of unclenching. Coordinate the gentle, deep breathing with the relaxation. As you inhale, your muscles will tense up.

3.   Relax and unclench every muscle on the out-breath. Move from the toes over the arch of the foot to the ankle, relaxing and unclenching each muscle and joint

coordinated with your breathing. Proceed up the calves, to the knee, then the thighs to the left hip. Now back to the right foot, relaxing and unclenching until the right hip is reached.

4.   Slowly relax the pelvis and groin then move up the front of the body, relaxing and unclenching with the out-breath until the neck is reached. Go back to the buttocks and move up the back of the body, relaxing every muscle in the back. Now move down each arm, from the shoulder to the fingertips, taking care to relax each finger and thumb. Relax and unclench the neck, up to the back of the head across the top and down over the face, checking that the teeth are unclenched and that the jaw is relaxed. Finally, make a quick scan of the whole body and relax any part that feels tense. Meditate on this state for a few minutes.

A Sanctuary Meditation

Every time a distracting thought enters your awareness while doing this meditation, simply say the word "stop." You may say it aloud or silently to yourself. This functions to dissipate the thought without diverting your attention and creating an emotional response. The following meditation will help you to attain this goal and further prepare you to experience advance levels of relaxation and spiritual growth:

1.   Sit comfortably with your back straight, apply protection and breathe deeply for one minute. Say to yourself, "I am totally relaxed," and let your mind create an ideal place of relaxation (a sanctuary).

2.   There are no responsibilities, tedious chores or distractions in your sanctuary. Remain in this place for a minimum of five minutes.

3.   Mentally return to the room where you are meditating and take a deep breath to go even deeper into this relaxed state. Any extraneous thoughts that may be encountered are to be immediately neutralized by saying "stop." Stay with this process for 15 minutes saying "stop" every time a distracting thought enters your mind.

An Eastern Meditation

Many people find solace and hope in meditating on a passage from their holy scriptures. Try this excerpt from the Hindu sacred writings:

"A leaf, a flower, a fruit, or even
Water, offered to me in devotion,
I will accept as the loving gift
Of a dedicated heart. Whatever you do,
Make it an offering to me.
The food you eat or worship you perform,
The help you give, even your suffering.
Thus you will be free from karma's bondage.
From the results of action, good and bad.
I am the same to all beings. My love
Is the same always. Nevertheless, those
Who meditate on me with devotion,
They dwell in me, and I shine forth in them.
Even the worst sinner becomes a saint

When he loves me with all his heart. This love
Will soon transform his personality
And fill his heart with peace profound.
This is my promise, O son of Kunti:
Those who love me, they shall never perish.

Even those who are handicapped by birth
Have reached the supreme goal of life
By taking refuge in me. How much more
The pure brahmins and royal sages who love me!

Give not your love to this transient world
Of suffering, but give all your love to me.
Give me your mind, your heart, all your worship.
Long for me always, live for me always,
And you shall be united with me."[2]

A Meditation on Death

Death, as we consider it, is a necessary transition to make
before ascension can be realized. There is no need to look
upon this state with sorrow or fear. How we live each day and
our level of spiritual evolvement determines our ability to
attain enlightenment and ascend following this physical
sojourn.

We all have the potential for developing and exhibiting
clarity, compassion, love and wisdom. Clinging to our
physical lives and manifesting fears and codependencies
prevent us from reaching this perfect state that is the basis of
this book.

---

[2] Bhagavad Gita, 9:26-34

Practice the following meditation to facilitate your own spiritual growth and to desensitize your fear of death.

1. Assume a comfortable position, relax and breathe deeply. Focus your attention on your body components one by one and contemplate their shape, size, function and nature.

2. Now move your attention to the inner workings of each cell of your body. Consider the fact that each cell is produced, functions for a short period of time, dies and is replaced by your DNA.

3. Shift your focus to your subconscious. Pay attention to its ability to store countless bits of data relating to your daily exposure to and expression of perceptions, thoughts and feelings. Follow this mechanism from the moment you wake up until you go to sleep.

4. Become aware of your current physical environment now. Note the room in which you are practicing this meditation, the ceiling, walls, floor, furniture, pictures and other components in this room.

5. Now move your focus to the rest of your home or apartment. Overview your neighborhood, with its people, pets and other structures. Stay with this thought for a few minutes.

6. Contemplate the idea that each of the images and thoughts you have focused on changes. Nothing lasts forever except our soul. People move and eventually die. What is beautiful today deteriorates with time. The difficulties and ugliness in things we sense today may appear as the reverse in the future.

7.   End this meditation with a positive view of psychic empowerment. Be optimistic about life and your destiny. There is no need to cling to physical life, as with all things it is transient.

The Transformation Meditation

There are always people in our lives who appear as antagonists or enemies. We have a natural tendency to hate or fear them. This prevents our spiritual growth. The purpose of this meditation is to transform these enemies into allies. We will also deal with neutral strangers in our world and learn how to convert them into friends.

1.   Assume a comfortable position, relax and breathe deeply. Visualize three people in your room: A friend, someone you dislike and a complete stranger.

2.   Focus your attention on your friend. Magnify the positive feelings you have for him or her, and sense the support this friend sends to you. Immerse yourself in the conviction that you wish only the best for this person.

3.   Shift your attention to the individual you currently consider as an enemy. Elaborate how this person attempts to hurt you, irritates you and makes you feel angry or afraid. Immerse yourself in a global assessment of this person.

4.   Move your attention to the complete stranger. Contemplate your feelings of indifference toward this person. Concentrate on the fact that the basis of your feelings for these three people is affected by their

attitude and actions toward you at this point in time.

5.   Return your focus to your friend and create a
     circumstance in which this friend turns against you and
     is now your enemy. Concentrate on your feelings of
     hurt, disappointment and resentment. Remove any
     negative energy toward and from this person. Wish the
     friend well but remove this person from your life.

6.   Now concentrate on your enemy and imagine this
     person becoming your friend. Focus on your feelings
     of love and kindness toward this former enemy. This
     new friend has replaced your former friend in your
     heart.

7.   Consider the stranger now. Understand how one act
     could transform this person into either a friend or
     enemy. Create a situation in which this individual is
     drawn close to you and is now your friend.
     Concentrate on the love and support you each have for
     each other.

8.   Finally reconsider your former friend who has become
     an enemy. By sending love, that person has lost hate
     for you and has once again become your friend.
     Visualize yourself projecting love, compassion and
     support for this person once again.

9.   Reflect on these three people simultaneously, whereas
     originally one was a friend, one an enemy and one a
     stranger, now all three are your friends. Consider the
     principle that everyone deserves our love and
     compassion. It is our narrowminded prejudices that
     create negativity in our lives. We are all God's
     creation.

A Love Meditation

To be truly evolved spiritually requires the ability to send loving energy to everyone. This meditation assists us in developing our natural desire to love all things and to express that feeling freely and unconditionally.

1.   Assume a comfortable position, relax and breathe deeply. First focus on all of the people and things in your life you love. Include your pets, hobbies, favorite restaurants, music, movies and so on. Magnify this feeling of total love.

2.   Now bring into this picture people and things that you dislike and include feelings of hatred if they are relevant. Concentrate for a moment on your desire to be able to love these other people and things, that you currently dislike or hate, in the same manner as the first group.

3.   Create a feeling of love in your heart for every person and item represented by this entire picture. Treat all members of this personal world of yours with the same unconditional love. This feeling of love may be visualized as a radiating bright white or gold light of pure and positive energy emanating form your heart.

4.   Accept all persons and things in this scene for who or what they are, with each of their faults as well as good points. Radiate out from your heart this bright light so that it both touches and surrounds every component of this scene.

5.   Say to each person, "May my love become yours, and may you be fulfilled in all your desires. Live long and

may you attain your own enlightenment at the end of this life to ascend to be with God."

6. Continue sending out this loving light and observe its effects on others. See how each person is transformed into a loving entity. Note how the things you disliked before (food, places, music, etc.) all of a sudden become a positive force in your life.

7. Contemplate how you now have the potential to love people and things equally. Dedicate your consciousness to remove any aspect of your personality, such as impatience, superficiality, anger, jealousy, insecurity, and so on, that stands in the way of this unconditional love. Stay with this goal for a few minutes.

A Compassion Meditation

For this meditation I recommend the use of a mantra. A mantra may be defined as a series of syllables that corresponds to certain energy frequencies within our consciousness. The effectiveness of a mantra lies in our concentrating on its sound as we recite it aloud or silently.

There are many mantras to choose from. Christians often select a prayer to Jesus, such as "Lord Jesus Christ, Son of God, have mercy on us." Saint Theresa of Avila used the following mantra:

"Let nothing upset you;
Let nothing frighten you.
Everything is changing;
God alone is changeless.
Patience attains the goal.

Who has God lacks nothing:
God alone fills all our needs."

Jews have often uttered, "Barukh attah Adonai, Blessed are thou, oh Lord." Muslims have used the mantra, "Allahu akbar. God is great," or simply, "Allah, Allah." "Om mani padme hum" (pronounced om mah-nee ped-may hoom), used by Buddhists for centuries, signifies "the jewel in the lotus of the heart." This mantra expresses the pure energy of compassion that exists in every being. Another Indian mantra is:

"Hare Rama Hare Rama
Rama Rama Hare Hare
Hare Krishna Hare Krishna
Krishna Krishna Hare Hare."

1. Assume a comfortable position, relax and breathe deeply. Concentrate on the loving radiant light you created in the previous meditation. Make this light a different color and have it now represent compassion. Recite your mantra.

2. Concentrate on those people closest to you who are suffering in some way. Open your heart to the physical and psychological problems they are experiencing and think that just like you, they want to be free of all suffering. Feel how wonderful it would be if they were free and could enjoy the peace and bliss of enlightenment. Recite your mantra. Expand your compassion-radiating light to surround them and visualize this helping to relieve their suffering. Recite

your mantra.

3. Now focus on people who have done unkind things to you, and to whom you harbored resentment and anger. Concentrate on their suffering: physical pain and discomfort, feelings of loneliness, insecurity, fear, dissatisfaction. Send out your light of compassion to these individuals and open your heart to these people for whom normally you feel irritation or anger. Recite your mantra. Observe how their suffering is eased.

4. Concentrate on people you don't know around your community who are also suffering. Again visualize your light of compassion to emanate from your heart and facilitate an end to their suffering. Recite your mantra.

5. Repeat step 4, only now expand this scene to include people from all around the world.

6. Focus your complete attention on your light of compassion, and affirm to your Higher Self that you will overcome your negative energy and develop pure love and compassion for all beings. Feel that you are connecting with your own Higher Self and pure loving consciousness. Your body feels light and blissful, your mind peaceful and clear. The compassion light from your heart radiates out to every living being, purifying their negative energy and filling them with bliss.

Purification Meditation

To purify our soul we must let go of all mistakes and problems, seeing them as temporary obscurations, not as an intrinsic part of our nature. It helps us get in touch with and develop our natural good energy.

1.   Assume a comfortable position, relax and breathe deeply. Visualize a bright white light above your head. This light is that of goodness, love and wisdom: the fulfillment of your own highest potential. Your Higher Self is represented by this bright white light.

2.   Imagine this light descends through your crown chakra and moves down to the third-eye chakra, into your throat chakra and finally enters your heart chakra. Meditate on this for a few moments.

3.   Now radiate this loving light of your Higher Self to encompass your entire physical body. Your physical body dissolves and becomes light; each component of your body is transformed into pure white light. Concentrate on all of your negative thoughts, feelings and behaviors and have them dissolve into a black void. What is left is a state of perfection and wholeness represented by this white light of your merging with your Higher Self.

4.   Enjoy this feeling of joy and empowerment. If any thought or distracting object should appear in your mind, let it also dissolve into white light. Meditate in this way for a few minutes.

5.   Now concentrate on your breathing. As you inhale back in your physical body, create an image of white light representing pure energy that is loving and positive. This white light permeates every fiber of your body, bringing with it feelings of protection, love, compassion, wisdom and bliss.

6.   As you exhale, imagine that all your negative energy, past mistakes, distorted conceptions and emotions leave your body with the breath. Visualize this energy as a black void and send it out into space, where it disappears completely. Feel confident that you have freed yourself from every trace of faults and negativity. From this moment on you will transform all negativity into this black void and literally breathe these obstacles to your enlightenment out into oblivion. Concentrate on this for a few minutes.

A Forgiveness Meditation

We can take great strides in healing old hurts that block our ability to trust in ourselves and others by learning to forgive. Forgiveness opens up our heart to spiritual growth and facilitates our path to ascension.

1.   Assume a comfortable position, relax and breathe deeply. Allow your mind to bring up past memories of things you have said, thought or did that you would like to forgive. Concentrate on the feelings and images associated with these past issues and let them float freely in your mind.

2.   Now say to yourself, "I forgive myself completely for everything I have both intentionally and unintentionally done. My heart is open to receive the pure love, strength and the ability to forgive from my Higher Self. May I be able to share this gift with others, and assist them in their own forgiveness."

3.   Visualize someone in your life currently whose

forgiveness you seek, or whom you want to forgive. Say to this person, "I forgive you for any of your past actions and intentions. May your life be filled with light, joy and peace. I ask your forgiveness for anything I may have done to you in the past. May we both grow as a result of this forgiveness and learn to love each other unconditionally."

4.   Now focus on this message being both received and accepted. Meditate on this for a few minutes.

5.   Repeat steps 3 and 4, only now concentrate on someone toward whom you feel anger, resentment, hatred or any other form of negativity.

6.   Shift your focus now to those individuals in the past for whom you have negative feelings. Repeat steps 3 and 4 and end by meditating on this forgiveness for a few minutes.

7.   Finally, imagine a feeling of release, love and growth surrounding your entire being as a result of this ability to forgive yourself and others.

A Wisdom Meditation

1.   Assume a comfortable position, relax and breathe deeply. Visualize a bright white light above your head filled with the knowledge and wisdom of the universe. This is your Higher Self.

2.   Perceive this white light entering the top of your head through your crown chakra and filling your entire body. Each and every one of your seven major chakras are immersed with this white light and its wisdom.

3.   Focus on a question about your karmic purpose, or

anything that you would like to know, and let this light of wisdom telepathically answer your question and transfer its wisdom to your subconscious. Meditate on this for a few minutes.

4.   Now remove all thoughts about the physical world and merge with this white light of wisdom. You may notice colors, sounds and other phenomena around you begin to dissolve and merge with this white light. Leave your physical body and become this white light of wisdom. Meditate on this for a few minutes.

5.   When you are ready open up your eyes and breathe normally.

A Final Comment About Meditation and Spiritual Growth

These exercises are designed to facilitate your spiritual growth and prepare you for ascension. There are other things and lifestyle changes you can do now to de-stress your life and quicken the rate of your spiritual growth. Here are some helpful suggestions:

1.   Prioritize your life and do only the most important things first.

2.   Take frequent breaks and practice meditation or self-hypnosis daily.

3.   Spend a few moments each day observing nature. Stop and smell the roses.

4.   Learn to delegate tasks.

5.   Maintain your sense of humor.

6.   Overcome any tendency to procrastinate.

7.   Always try to learn from any situation, regardless of how positive or negative it may appear to be.

8.   Practice focusing your concentration on one thing at a time. Complete your tasks with more awareness, thoroughness and respect.

9.   Allow some time in your day to be alone with your thoughts. Always keep an optimistic viewpoint with issues you are contemplating.

10.   Schedule at least one pleasurable activity in your life daily.

11.   Be assertive and learn to say no to someone you care for when asked to do something you don't want to do.

12.   Incorporate exercise and a good diet into your life. For details on this I suggest my book, "Look Younger, Live Longer Naturally."[3]

13.   Be loving, unselfish and kind. Love is the most important quality in the universe.

14.   Be a giver. Eliminate the tendency to take from others. Live a more simple and quality life.

15.   Decrease the attachment to material possessions. Enjoy them all you want but be willing to lose them without envy, resentment, anger or other negative emotional responses.

16.   Be empowered. You may want certain things out of life but never be needy.

17.   Be God-oriented instead of world-oriented.

18.   Be humble. Eliminate the desire to be ruthless,

---

[3] B. Goldberg, "Look Younger, Live Longer Naturally: (St. Paul: Llewellyn, 1998).

aggressive and conceited. Remove all tendencies to be superficial, vain and phony.

19. Learn not to identify too strongly with your body. Say to yourself, "I am a spiritual soul, immortal and eternal. I create my own reality." The body eventually dies, but the soul is eternal.

Chapter 8:
The Changing Universe

*T*he universe we live in is incomplete. As long as we reside in the lower five planes, our mind creates a reality from the perspective of an imperfect soul. Our natural dysfunction to impose self-centeredness and evil onto our creation makes it stressful and far less fulfilling than the higher planes.

All that we know of, due to our five senses, is in a constant state of flux. It is our state of consciousness that determines the world we perceive. We can only witness a change in our realm by creating it within our own consciousness.

It may be comforting to some to acknowledge this godlike power of creation. Bear in mind that we are far from perfect, and create a world with many problems. The only utopia that exists is on the higher planes, where the soul is pure and cause and effect ceases to be a factor.

Being the master of our own universe, and combining this function with spiritual perfection, has many implications on the universe as a whole. Our personal universe is but a microcosm of the whole universe, or macrocosm.

The better our microcosm universe functions, the more we add to the quality of the whole universe. We are master of our own destiny. There is no original sin, First Cause or anything else we can't overcome to achieve perfection. Our only limitations are those housed within our own consciousness.

These other planes that I described in Chapter 5 are realms containing an infinite number of states of consciousness. Our soul activates these other worlds. We are their reality. They couldn't exist without our creative gifts.

As each plane has an infinite number of possible experiences for our soul, we must use our good karmic sense in our choices, as well as our creations. When we travel to these other realms, as we will in Chapter 15, an adjustment is required to the environment and laws that are characteristic of these other dimensions.

We can easily make this adjustment. This is part of the reason our universe is constantly changing. This is due to the fact that our consciousness is continually in a state of flux. Spiritual growth and perfection become even more necessary as the only way we can ascend and prepare the path for others to return to God.

The first step in this changing universe is to already assume a state of God Awareness. By adopting this paradigm we send out this energy to others who we will attract into our sphere of influence. As like attract like, so will our world become more spiritual and more perfect.

This mind-meld must be absolute. You cannot simply hope that this will be so. You must live your life today within the heart of the God state to change your universe to allow for your own ascension. You are changing yourself by raising your soul's energy in the process of this transformation.

To assist us in our spiritual evolution and in better contributing to the changing universe, we may spiritually petition God. This process consists of four steps. The first step is simply to ask God for something that is currently beyond our own ability to obtain.

When Jesus said, "Seek, and ye shall find; knock and it shall be opened unto you," he was alluding to this principle. Unfortunately, most of the time our petition will remain unanswered. Our request cannot be granted unless we are spiritually evolved enough to receive it. This appears to be a catch-22 situation, but not if you continue to purify your soul.

Prayer is the second method of spiritually petitioning God. This stage is more powerful than the first method of simply asking God for something. The problem with this step is its co-dependency tendencies. Most prayers, as with most requests made to God, go unanswered.

We have discussed meditation at length in Chapter 7. This method represents the third method of spiritually petitioning God. The advantage of meditation is that it can be part of a program of psychic empowerment, and coupled with right living facilitates our spiritual path to perfection.

The fourth and final method to spiritually petition God is through self-hypnosis. In Chapter 13 I will present a thorough discussion with several exercises to illustrate this method of facilitating our path to enlightenment. Although not referenced per se in any scriptures as a method of spiritually petitioning God, we will shortly see that it is by far the most efficient method.

We must always remember that even though our universe is continually changing, the total amount of energy in it remains constant. Energy may be transformed as electrical energy becomes light energy, but nothing is lost during this process.

Our soul is energy in the form of electromagnetic radiation. Television or radio signals are other examples of this type of energy. We can never lose the energy contained in our soul. Techniques are available to us to raise the quality, not quantity, of our soul's energy to allow us to ascend. This technique is called cleansing and will be discussed in Chapter 13.

The fact that we have free will and individual freedom is critical to surviving and thriving in this changing universe. We must rise above the illusions of the material world, and the temptation to follow other paradigms and/or actions of those less spiritual in order to eliminate the need to remain with the karmic cycle.

Honesty with ourselves and pure motives assist us in our spiritual endeavors. Along with these pure intentions we must learn to discriminate between truth and illusion. Do not expect to see perfection in yourself until you are able to see the infinite God in all that you encounter. By exhibiting charity, freedom, compassion, love and wisdom we can all attain enlightenment.

Our soul's energy has a Higher Self perfect counterpart, which emanates from God. This divine spark within us makes us able to become one with God, and ascension is the mechanism by which that is manifested.

Demonstrating charity, freedom, compassion, love and wisdom allows us to grow in our changing universe. It requires a detachment from the material world. Obsessions with possessions or clinging to loved ones because of insecurities will hold us back from atonement.

By detachment I am not suggesting we all take a vow of

poverty. I am implying that our attention should always be directed at reaching the God plane. All decisions should be made from a spiritual perspective. When we want nothing we receive everything. Desire is the source of all pain.

The opposite is also true. When we need something we usually receive nothing but rejection for our efforts. Desire is a need, and it is controlled by the illusionary forces of the physical plane. This negative force uses our mind to dominate and control us only if we allow it.

Yin and Yang polarities of ancient Chinese philosophy illustrate this principle. The Taoist concept of polarities states that nothing can exist except in relation to its opposite. Yin is the concrete, material world, whereas Yang represents the abstract, spiritual realm.

The negative Yin is the ability to adapt and lives in the physical plane. Yang represents the positive and strength components of our soul. Nothing is ever entirely Yin or Yang. The ability of all aspects of our universe to change, including the universe itself, is demonstrated by this ancient Chinese philosophy.

A proper balance of Yin and Yang keeps us healthy physically, emotionally, mentally and spiritually. The universe may be constantly changing, but as long as we grow spiritually we can change along with it and stay ahead of its evolvement so that we may move onto the higher realms it offers.

The Neoplatonist Plotinus (A.D. 205-270) presented the concept of an "intellectual cosmos." He thought that we each have many levels on which our soul can experience the universe. We all select the level (plane) in which we reside. Our Higher Self exists on the level above the one we have chosen. As we rise in spiritual evolution, this Higher Self follows us, always remaining on the plane above us. He stated, "Our guardian is the next higher faculty of our being. . . . Our guardian is both related to us and independent of us. . . . Our guardian helps us to carry out the destiny we have chosen."[1]

When we speak of these other dimensions it is interesting to note how they have been depicted throughout history. Pope Gregory the Great was asked many times about the fact that dying people sometimes perceived a ship coming to take them to the Otherworld. Gregory stated, "The soul needs no vehicle, but it is not surprising that, to a man still placed within his body, there should appear that which he is used to seeing by means of his body, so that he might in this way comprehend where his soul might be taken spiritually."[2]

We face a dilemma as a soul living on the physical plane. Many of our theologies do not properly prepare us for enlightenment. To do so involves attaining a certain wholeness and atonement. Religions foster a codependency relationship in which they function as agents to connect us to God. Isn't that why we possess a Higher Self?

In order to understand our essence in relation to this changing universe we live in, let us combine physics and cosmic consciousness. Consider the various levels of being and consciousness as colors in the spectrum of light. Although each specific color appears somewhat different, all colors are

---

[1] Plotinus, "Enneads," Trans. Kenneth Guthrie (London: George Bell and Sons, 1918), I:235-39.
[2] Pope Gregory the Great, "Dialogues" (quoted in Jacques LeGoff, "The Birth of Purgatory," trans. Arthur Goldhammer [Chicago: University of Chicago Press, 1984], 206).

part of a single band of white light.

Our soul is a multilevel manifestation of the single Consciousness of God, and has descended down to the physical plane through several gradations to the identity with which we have come to know it. This is why mysticism is defined as the experience of direct communication with ultimate reality.

Wilbur stated this concept succinctly when he averred, "The process of psychological development proceeds in a most articulate fashion. At each stage, a higher-order structure—more complex and therefore more unified—is introduced to consciousness, and eventually . . . the self identifies with that emergent structure. For example, . . . as language emerged in consciousness, the self began to shift from a solely biological bodyself to a syntaxical ego. . . . It was then no longer bound exclusively to the body, but it was bound to the mental-ego. . . . As evolution proceeds, however, each level in turn is differentiated from the self, or 'peeled off' so to speak. The self eventually disidentifies with its present structure so as to identify with the next higher-order emergent structure. . . . It doesn't throw that [lower] structure away, it simply no longer exclusively identifies with it. . . . [In this way] (1) what is whole becomes part; (2) what is identification becomes detachment; (3) what is context becomes content. . . . (4) what is ground becomes figure. . . . Each of those points is, in effect, a definition of transcendence. Yet each is also a definition of a stage of development. It follows that the two are essentially identical."[3]

We can summarize this chapter's theme by stating that our

---

[3] K. Wilbur, "The Atman Projection" (Wheaton, IL: Theosophical Pub., 1980).

consciousness exists in a changing universe, and the constitution of our soul is on a spectrum along with our Higher Self. Although our Higher Self is always situated one plane above us, it can communicate with us daily.

The fact that we have different levels of consciousness makes it possible to distinguish between regular knowledge and true wisdom from our Higher Self.

This distinction is important not in order to advocate duality but to discover where each is appropriate. Such a distinction is critical in an attempt to specify how to achieve ascension in an ever changing universe. The continuum of consciousness and the relationship between stages of development and stages of transcendence suggest that there may be a regular interaction between the everyday and the other spiritual dimensions.

_____

*O*ur soul has both a physical embodiment and a spiritual home. One consequence of this tension is ambivalence. We simultaneously feel pulled between the extremes of freedom and commitment, merging and separation, sexual indulgence and abstinence, and fusion and differentiation. We are troubled by this polarity of desiring to rise above the experience of the material world, yet live as fully as possible.

We must understand the calling of our soul to be able to return to God. Our karmic purpose is why we chose the physical plane to learn the lessons necessary for our spiritual growth. Though once pure Spirit, the soul becomes "human," a word that derives from the Latin humus, meaning earth. As the soul becomes involved with life on this physical plane, it is easily diverted from its spiritual path. As we grow more entangled in secular living, our vision grows dimmer, and so our behavior is likely to stray farther and farther from the reason we incarnated. For example, living off a family inheritance is easier than exerting oneself to build a career that expresses one's soul's purpose.

I have presented the principles of karma several times already in this book. A further discussion of this ancient doctrine is necessary in order to comprehend the obstacles in ascension.

Karma is simply the sum total of the consequences of all our actions. Some have good consequences while some ill-conceived actions have harmful consequences. Regardless of whether our actions create positive or negative karma, the law of karma assures that we must experience the return of the effects of our actions.

Karma functions as a feedback system that permits us to become aware of our actions and to learn from them. Negative karma is generated by repeatedly going against our soul's purpose. Continued creation of bad karma forces us to lose sight of any aspect of our karmic purpose.

As bad karma intensifies, we grow increasingly more frustrated. This weight may manifest in a number of ways depending on a person's vulnerabilities as chronic or life-threatening diseases, or as reduced effectiveness and vitality. Whatever the form, the soul loses its light and the person loses contact with the soul.

Spiritual growth achieved by any means brings into play the fact that karma also has the potential for promoting growth. By living with increasing sensitivity to the effects of our actions upon others and upon life, we can deliberately set out to act in ways that further life and thereby bring good karma. Because we also reap the sowing of these positive actions, we gain an uplifting momentum. We can also find ways to transmute or balance any negative karma perhaps by entering the spiritual path or serving others.

At almost any point in life, we can attain such a compelling awareness of our soul's calling as to consciously invite the clearing of bad karma by active transmutation, rather than passively awaiting its return. The moment this occurs our soul begins to reverse the long process down into immanence, shifts its emphasis to the process of transcendence, and begin the uphill trek home to God.

Ancient writings inform us that our soul undergoes the same energy transformation as that of the Prima Materia in the alchemical tradition. According to the teachings of alchemy, energy journeys from undifferentiated wholeness, through separation, to a new wholeness which is now differentiated and conscious. As the Prima Materia spirals into its separation from the original Source, the Prima Materia precipitates as a physical world. As the material world in turn spirals back toward its Source through ascending stages of purification and etherealization, it becomes spiritualized.

The soul is situated midway between heaven and earth, between immanence and transcendence, between cosmic origin and dense embodiment. Our energy essence gravitates in two different directions. The soul is involved in a process of spiraling back and forth between the two realms. Our goal is to redirect it to the path back to God.

The Neoplatonist Plotinus alluded to ascension when he stated, "We must close our eyes and invoke a new manner of seeing . . . a wakefulness that is the birthright of us all, though few put it to use."[1] Throughout history this principle has been alluded to, although often disguised in symbolic form.

---

[1] Plotinus, "The Essential Plotinus." Trans. E. O'Brien (Indianapolis: Hackett, 1964) p. 42.

The Hermetic Marriage

In discussing our return to God by ascension, or stairway to heaven, the paradigms of Hermes Trismegistus, the ancient Egyptian god of wisdom, learning, literature and science, must be once again presented. We discussed Hermes in detail in Chapter 2.

The name Hermes was given to the Egyptian bird-headed Thoth by the ancient Greeks. He was known to ancient Masonry as the cosmic fire, Chiram, and as Hiram Abiff later on. One component of Hermes's metaphysics that is of interest to us at this time is the Hermetic marriage.

Alchemy is a basic principle professed in Hermetic writings. We are said to contain within ourselves all the elements of Nature, both human and divine. As the alchemists claimed to be able to transform lead into gold, we have the capability to transform our human nature into a spiritual gold through the mechanism of our soul.

Everything in nature is alive, according to the ancients. Only Christianity denies this concept and maintains a separation of God from His creation. The Jews, Chinese, Persians and Brahmans have depicted God as being involved with our very being. Man dwells in God, and it is through this connection that we have being.

The Hermetists clearly state, "Man, know thyself! For thou, like God, art all wisdom and all power and art the shadow being witness unto the Eternal."[2] These ancients consider all elements of nature (the minerals, the air, the Earth itself) as living things, endowed by God with feelings, intelligence and consciousness.

---

[2] Hermes Trismegistus, op. cit.

The spirit of man is the divine spark containing the power of creating its immortality. This ability to ascend is called the Causal Man by the ancients and denotes an ability to deliver our soul from its temporary home on the physical plane back to God, our source. The central cohesive power that binds us together is this spirit or soul.

The Hermetic Marriage as depicted from the romance of the spiritual and the material is best reflected in the New Testament's Book of Revelation. Jerusalem is depicted as a bridge, married to the Lamb. The four hills on which Jerusalem is built are cabalistically the four beasts of Ezekiel, the four aspects of the Egyptian sphynx, the four heads of Brahma and the four bodies of man (physical, astral, mental and causal).[3]

Most of us view our physical body as a prison, making ascension almost impossible. We feel frustrated by not being . able to describe the beauty we see or feel. Sometimes we hear a song but cannot reproduce it. The list is endless.

As a spiritually evolved soul, however, we never lose hope, and look within for our own ability to attain liberation. To use the analogy of the Hermetic Marriage, our physical body becomes the city of our soul. When it is cleansed and purified, it dons its wedding garment and becomes the bride of the spirit.

This regenerated body is the robe of the high priest. It is now the golden wedding garment of St. Paul, without which the disciple is not permitted entry into the wedding feast of the Lamb.

---

[3] There is a fifth body known as the etheric in many systems of metaphysics.

The Steps on the Staircase to Heaven

To attain God-realization we must acquire faith, knowing and experience. Without the requisite experience, knowing, faith and realization are impossible. Each of these factors is but a step on the staircase to heaven.

Think about a sport you may be interested in. For example, let's assume you want to master tennis. You can read all the books in this field, watch videos and attend matches. Until you step on the court with racket in hand and play (experience), you will not be able to play the game.

The same principle applies to God-realization. It is not enough simply to read books on ascension, such as this one, you must obtain experience. Fortunately, I have provided dozens of exercises to assist you in your spiritual endeavors.

God-realization is nothing but a concept, a hypothetical, until you actually experience your Higher Self and experience soul purification. In Chapter 13 I will describe this cleansing process in detail.

Knowledge and knowing are not the same thing. To obtain knowledge is relatively easy. All we have to do is read and fill our minds with data. But this is only information. Possessing this knowledge does not automatically mean that you can apply it to life. The experiences of life transform this knowledge into a knowing of how to incorporate the raw data to our soul's growth.

Faith in what we experience is the next step in the stairway to heaven. We must have the confidence to trust our inner self to accept our experiences as valid. When we master this concept of faith, the combination of experience and knowing prepares us for God-realization. It is only through direct personal experience that we will find our way back to God.

You will observe an elimination of any previous fears of death when you encounter adventures out of the body, as I present in Chapter 13. By realizing through personal experiences that you do live beyond the physical body, you are released from the bondage of the fear of death.

When you exhibit a knowing that you are a creative part of God, you encourage the development of love in your life. This is accompanied by an inner fulfillment that overcomes previous feelings of loneliness or alienation.

This in turn fosters your faith in your spiritual purpose, and fills you with joy and excitement. All guilt is eliminated and this newfound strength makes it easier to serve others without being concerned with your own previous limitations.

To finally realize that our destiny is to become a co-worker with God differentiates this God-realization from Hinduism or Buddhism. In these theologies, our ultimate destiny as individuals is a dissolution of our separate identity and a merging with the God energy.

Love

Love is a most unusual aspect of our being. We often do not notice it at first, but when it grows and finally expresses itself we are surprised. Love is an emotion that gradually expands our consciousness and flows out to the world, changing others around us.

God is the origin of our love. This dynamic force of good and beauty becomes a spiritual force within us, if we allow it. The power of love is much stronger than that of our conscious mind. Love can overcome just about any obstacle because of its faith and compassion components. This awakening has to start within one's heart. The result of giving love is an introduction to a greater awareness, and a movement from one world to the next and into the higher plane of God-realization.

Barriers to Ascension

One of the strongest obstacles to the path back to God is our ego. These defense mechanisms represent such things as vanity and prejudices. When we allow too much of our personality to interfere with our experiences and spiritual growth, we can place far greater emphasis upon the vehicle of expression of truth rather than the ultimate truth itself.

This is one of the repeated errors we have made in looking externally to others for our salvation. Too often the personality of a leader convinces us that he or she is the true bearer of the truth. No true spiritual leaders are known for their personality, but the fact that they are merely an instrument for truth.

Personality has its own hidden problems. For example, many charismatic leaders assume they possess a certain degree of infallibility, and profess their virtues by pointing out the faults of others. This overinflated ego and insecure approach is hardly going to unveil the ultimate truth.

The fact that we seek the truth from outside sources defeats the very theme of this book. We have free will, and only we can function as the vessel for our ultimate truth and path back to God. We must focus our efforts on seeking truth as a quality rather than as a personality or thing.

One sign that we are entering the ascension path is an internally generated awakening. The ancients taught that truth is that which is. There are no artificial qualifications for this truth, and our attempts to bestow such prerequisites manifest as among the greatest obstacles in our path to ascension. It is all too easy to confuse truth with the messenger, and allow ourselves to be swayed by the messenger's personality.

There is nothing really wrong with a messenger projecting a dynamic personality. The key is always in the message. If these individuals attempt to accumulate followers and prescribe the way to God by their paradigms, watch out. On the other hand, an encouragement to look within ourselves to our own perfect Higher Self (or whatever name you want to call it) is far more likely to result in attaining spiritual perfection.

Western society is much too verbal in its orientation. Words alone will not result in ascension. Any symbol or illustration requires some physical means of expression to appeal to our five senses. Following these words alone subjects us to the limitations imposed by the physical plane.

The ultimate truth requires an awakening within our very being. This experience, knowing, faith and God-realization is not subject to our physical laws. A raise in consciousness cannot be attained by some cookbook approach. If that were possible, the Mystery Schools and all the other religions I discussed in Chapter 3 would have succeeded in training their followers to ascend.

As I have previously stated, very few souls have actually ascended. The great majority of us reincarnate over and over again into more dysfunctional lives. If you question my analysis of society, look around and compare our present circumstances to 20, 30, 50 or 100 years ago. My reading of history shows every possible sign of moral decay and dysfunctional behavior has increased within the last 30 years alone.

You may argue this point, but you can't deny the facts. Drug use is up, divorce rates are well over 50 percent, crime is out of control and morality seems to be disappearing into the vortex of the space-time continuum.

I am not a pessimist. My cup isn't half empty or half full, it's overflowing. But I cannot ignore the reality of what my physical senses observe. There is hope, but it will not be through a repetition of old paradigms that simply do not work.

We must learn to guide ourselves into a higher state of consciousness that will allow us to ascend the staircase to heaven and return to God. No teacher or book can do this for us. All our problems are self-created. When we open ourselves to our Higher Self and allow our natural divine spark to stimulate our awakening, we have taken the first step on the path to nirvana.

Soon, by applying the techniques presented in this book and following the instructions of your own Higher Self, you will finally come to the realization and knowing that everything you experience is designed to provide opportunities for your spiritual growth. At the end of this ascension path is an overwhelming state of love for all other beings, ourselves and God.

I n our individual path to ascension we are tested according to the level of spiritual growth we have attained. None of us is tested beyond our spiritual capacity. It is at the weakest line in our spiritual makeup, or most vulnerable areas, that we experience the greatest degree of difficulty.

You and I have a different state of consciousness. Every person on this planet, as well as those occupying the other planes, possess a different frequency vibrational rate, or level of spiritual growth. This level of spiritual evolvement is determined by our past-life karmic tests, and the experience we have in our current lifetime.

Each of us is responsible for our own spiritual evolution. This responsibility is actually a key to spiritual freedom. Do not look upon it as an obstacle. Part of our karmic purpose and place in God's universe is to both possess and exercise free will. Free will is a responsibility.

We create our own reality. Those of you that favor hard science paradigms will find it supportive to know that the hard science known as quantum physics mathematically demonstrates this fact. It is by taking responsibility for our actions that we earn spiritual maturity and are assured a place on the path toward ascension. I refer to this principle as psychic empowerment.

By accessing your Higher Self you are allowing God more fully into your life. Divine love accompanies this divine presence. The richness and joy of life become evident as God awakens your heart through the mediation of your Higher Self.

Now you can begin to see cycles and connections between your current and past lives and eternal wisdom. This is part of the knowing I alluded to in Chapter 9. An opening of your inner eyes and ears to the presence of the divine spark of God within us known as our Higher Self is the key to spiritual evolution.

Those souls who have mastered ascension techniques exhibit a different presence than most of us. Those God-realized souls have spiritually evolved, and we can learn from them what to expect when we reach this level.

Such an adept can accurately see the auras of others. They exhibit a degree of psychic development unknown to the average person. Telepathy, telekinesis, precognition, out-of-body travel are mere child's play to these souls.

One important feature to note along the spiritual path is that the more we become evolved, the less attachment we have to material things. The presence and acceptance of God in our life remove all codependencies and insecurities. The illusory associations with the physical plane are no longer attractive.

The memory of our soul is perfect. It is eternal and can access the Akashic records to ascertain information concerning any past, present, parallel or future life. Part of God's wisdom is manifested in the fact that we enter into a new life freed of the memories of our prior existences. Can you imagine how difficult it would be to deal with these memories of thousands of lives at any moment? Most of us have enough difficulty keeping our current life in order.

Spiritual evolution allows us to handle this data, and this is why our psychic gifts are developed as our soul's energy raises its quality. We may feel depressed and experience suffering of various sorts, but our soul itself is always happy. It is an ethereal-like state, and composed of the same substance (although lower in quality) that constitutes our perfect Higher Self.

As we move closer to God-realization, our level of happiness and fulfillment increases on the soul level, as well as in the physical, mental and emotional aspects of our being. Our experience on the physical plane affords us with all the opportunities necessary for our spiritual growth. By growing in our inner consciousness, we no longer fear making mistakes, as we develop our faith in eventually being with God.

The spiritually evolving soul exhibits a noble character, characterized by a high ethical code, philosophic calm and inspired nature. It is moving to a state of ecstasy by way of the connection established with its consummate counterpart, the Higher Self.

A perfect interplay will now be established between the soul and the physical body. The difference between the outer material world of illusion and the true inner world of divine energy will be discerned. It is by strengthening this spiritual link to the God energy within us that will open us up to ascension.

Meditation and self-hypnosis exercises accelerate this path. It is no coincidence that these methods have been used since ancient times for spiritual evolution. There is no question about our ability to apply these simple and natural techniques to facilitate our spiritual growth. Practice and proper motivation are all that are required.

When I observe human nature I see two basic groups of people. One type follows the path of immediate gratification, self-indulgence and the philosophy or behavior of others. These groupies come in all shapes, sizes, races, creeds, educational backgrounds and socioeconomic strata.

We see celebrity groupies of all of all kinds, political groupies, intellectual groupies, athletic groupies and so on. The temptation to follow others is great, especially in a society that brainwashes us with its idea of suitable role models.

A spiritually evolved soul doesn't join groups or follow others. We take counsel with our inner consciousness, our Higher Self. When we listen to and enact the truth emanating from our soul, we function from a higher state of consciousness, and are indirectly directed by God. This is the second group of people.

As we spiritually evolve, certain characteristics become evident in our behavior. Forgiveness, love, contentment, unattachment, humility, discrimination and continence, to name a few, become part of our nature. Our attitude is relaxed, we take things lightly and project a happy outlook.

Many patients ask me why they cannot have direct contact with God now. The answer is simple. God will not communicate with an impure soul. When you reach the state of ascension, you are merging with the divine spark within your soul known as the Higher Self. You become your Higher Self, and your state is one of perfection. This purity, harmony, peace, calmness and quiet will now be receptive to and invite direct communication from God.

In Chapter 13, I will present several exercises to train you to leave the body and travel to other planes. My reason for providing these techniques is to both prepare you for the soul plane ascension technique and expose you to the wisdom available on each of these dimensions.

Out-of-body experiences (OBEs) will also introduce you to spirit guides and what are known as lords of the other planes. It is easy to see how ancient man confused these demiurges with the true God. In Chapter 5, I pointed out how the mental plane is the home of most of the Masters and gods of the more popular religions.

When ancient man traveled to these other planes, the exposure to these lords of these other dimensions would convince them that this was the true God. The problem with this hypothesis is that God does not reside on any of the five lower planes. This is why the scriptures of the various religions I summarized in Chapter 3 depict very different gods. Some express one god (monotheism), while others emphasize many gods (polytheism).

I am not attempting to tear down all established religions. My purpose is to expose you to a paradigm you may not have considered. Keep an open mind and let your inner consciousness direct you to the truth. Never look externally for the truth.

As you travel to these other realms your soul will begin to accommodate to these new and wondrous environments. This is part of spiritual evolution. No longer will you be prone to obsessive and other dysfunctional behavior. You will be free and comfortable in these other worlds.

It is not unusual for my patients to describe their OBE voyages as one of joy, light, beauty and bliss. The experience is like none they have ever encountered on the physical plane. Opening these inner channels provides a destination for our true consciousness.

As we manifest this soul travel, we become more open to spiritual illumination. This state of mind results in an enfoldment that is far beyond anything you have been exposed to. This is the cosmic consciousness and ecstasy that has been referenced throughout history.

I often use the expression "living in the state of spiritual consciousness" to describe the state of mind of super-consciousness. Sometimes this condition is experienced as infrequent insights. Later small flashes appear within our mind to create harmony in our lives. With time this develops into a blissful state during which all loneliness and fear disappear.

When we begin to merge our subconscious with the Higher Self within our very being, this unified consciousness accelerates the express of our spiritual unfoldment. With each passing day our newly discovered truth and love radiate around us. A greater, expanding flow of consciousness results.

This new unified consciousness acts like a current for the God energy to raise our spiritual level to new peaks. We are the instrument for this divine Higher Self spark that now functions as a suction bringing us to a level conducive to God-realization. A balance is established with our subconscious, and a new higher level of consciousness is then established.

We can see examples of this form of spiritual evolution in poetry. Many poets have been inspired to write poems that are prophetic, impart wisdom or simply exist to be appreciated.

Another example is mantras. Mantras are produced by a certain combination of words and vowels that bring about a raising of our consciousness. This is due to an elevation in the frequency vibrational rate of our soul's energy. The rhythm and sound that are produced affect the astral, etheric and mental bodies within and surround our being. We then ride this wave of energy to a higher level of consciousness.

Spiritual evolution is demonstrated throughout all the various scriptures we have today. The New Testament tells us that Jesus died for our sins, ascended and appeared to his disciples and others several times long after his physical death at Calvary. The psychic abilities we tend to be in awe of are easily manifested by spiritually evolved souls.

Throughout the Old Testament and New Testament different forms of psychic phenomena are presented. These range from clairvoyance and precognition to trumpet voices, levitation, and spirit writing. There are numerous instances of materialization. I state these facts only to point out that as your spiritual growth is fostered, psychic gifts will manifest.

In my Los Angeles practice I have countless examples of patients who describe OBEs, precognition and telepathy as they raise their consciousness.

Victor Hugo, in *Toilers of the Sea*, declared: "There are times when the unknown reveals itself to the spirit of man in visions. . . . Those that depart still remain near us—they are in a world of light; but they as tender witnesses hover about our world of darkness. Though invisible to some they are not absent. Sweet is their presence; holy is their converse with us. . . . The dead are invisible, but are not absent. . . . Death is the greatest of liberators, the highest step for those who have lived upon its heights; he who has been no more than virtuous on earth becomes beauteous; he who has been beauteous becomes sublime."[1]

It is important to remember that each of us at this particular time in history and in our own body and social circle are to be born and tested by the laws of karma. By overcoming the physical plane temptations, by rising above the day-to-day turmoil and helping others, the speed of our soul's progress is increased. And by taking a little time each day to meditate on things of the spirit, we can develop within ourselves the wisdom to help others through the obstacle course that we are all traveling together.

We are reborn in a certain way each day that we live for others rather than self. For this reason, it is never too soon to begin the process of daily rebirth. This truth is as old as time itself. Now is the time for all of us to begin our spiritual quest, for it is later than we think. Within each of us is a part of that divine power that reaches out to God. As we evolve spiritually, that divine spark grows until we become it.

Here is a letter I received from a patient who summarized her experiences with raising her soul's energy as a result of the techniques I present in Chapter 13:

"Thank you so much for the new life you have given me, the one I was meant to live, but didn't know how. You just don't know what's happening inside of me, and how I'm growing and changing.

I run into people whom I haven't seen in about a year and

---

[1] V. Hugo, "Toilers of the Sea." Trans. Isabel F. Hapgood (Milpitas, CA: Atlantean Press, 1993).

they don't recognize me! I'm talking about people I saw on a regular, weekly basis for a while and got to know reasonably well. What's really changed is something very deep inside of me that radiates on the outside like a whole new exquisitely beautiful being. It's a true inner beauty, which rises to the surface.

Sometimes I'm so overcome with gratitude that I start crying. I never knew life was so beautiful. I never knew we have such loving angels all around us, guarding us and rejoicing in our own divine light. I never knew I had a divine light! I spent so much of my life groping around in the dark side of my crap. Honestly, I didn't know what happiness really was.

Happiness is being free of yourself and your dark side. Happiness is living in the moment and enjoying life just for me. Happiness is finding love of myself and in God and in the angels, and not needing it from anyplace, anyone, or anything else. Happiness is being a whole person. Being a whole and happy person is true freedom.

You have given this to me."

*O*ne of the greatest obstacles to finding the path to God is indifference to the universe, and a feeling of alienation. Life is difficult on the physical plane, and frustration fosters giving in to temptations that divert us from this all important path.

Most people seem to want doctrines to be preached to them. This applies to religion, politics, government and corporations. For these philosophies to be accepted, they must fulfill an immediate hunger. A spiritual teaching needs to be agreeable on a personal level to be respected and followed.

The problem with this tendency is that it is external. In addition, a rejection of a paradigm because it doesn't satisfy the individual only leads to patronization by those that dish out these doctrines. Many of these approaches are characterized by appeals to emotions rather than true spirituality, frightening the parishioner with threats of eternal damnation that should be a sin in itself.

It is the ego that is being catered to by these preachings. Since the ego rejects anything that fails to provide immediate answers or assistance, true spiritual growth and entrance to a path to God is impossible. To be truly spiritual is to appeal to the divine spark within us known as the Higher Self.

Following false paradigms, or basing your beliefs merely

on the charisma of the messenger, will not lead to ascension. The television ministries and other representations of organized religion should be put on notice. Carefully and objectively try to evaluate what their message is appealing to.

Does the message cater to emotions such as fear? Is this doctrine fostered on your subconscious by a charismatic teacher? If you find yourself suffering in some way, as in feeling guilty because you don't follow some theology to the letter, something is wrong.

The paths to God, and there are several of them, should always develop feelings of love, tolerance, forgiveness and seeking grace from within. If a theology fails on any of these points, think twice about its value.

We have been brainwashed to accept teachings that go against our true nature and spiritual base because they foster fear and codependency. The natural tendency is to resist change and repeat old behavioral patterns. The path to God requires spiritual growth, and that entails change.

The main problem about true spiritual wisdom that leads us to a path to God is that it cannot so easily be expressed in words. It must be known by others from within their own soul. Those of us dominated by worldly attachments and generalized feelings of unhappiness will not be receptive to the true knowing and wisdom of spiritual instruction.

We all seek the attainment of illuminated insight, but this must come from within. The revelations that lead us to the path to God is one that we must discover ourselves. Only the truths that arise from within our very being will be of any value to us in directing our consciousness to this path.

The paths to God are a long and arduous route that can

only be shortened by spiritual evolution. Impatience must be resisted and overcome. Fear must be eliminated and temptations to act upon external influences need to be removed from our psyche.

Empty your mind of preconceived notions and prejudices. Put aside all former opinions you may have adopted from external teachings. Look up this path to God objectively with an open mind and heart. Eliminate all codependencies and material attachments as you seek this path.

Throughout history, conventional and unconventional religions have focused in on metaphysical speculations and appeals to our basic emotions and insecurities. Although these theologies may have served a purpose in days past, they are not open to competing philosophies.

God-realization can only be attained by advancing well beyond the limit of the physical plane. The soul travel exercises in Chapter 13 provide ample opportunity for this experience. Any state less than absolute God-realization is simply imaginary, imperfect and speculative.

This is not the path to God. The beliefs of churches, mystics and charismatic messengers would lead you to believe that their external approach results in eternal bliss. The reality is that the highest you could possibly travel is to the mental plane, more often the upper astral dimension.

Just look at the history of the Catholic Church as an example of a schism based theology. In 1527 the duke of Bourbon under Emperor Charles V was trying to remove Pope Clement VII from his papal throne. Humanism, with its atheistic base, was sweeping across Europe.

The Protestant Church was being formed by Martin

Luther, and Henry VIII broke with the Pope and created the Church of England. We also see the workings of Zwingli and John Calvin breaking off form Catholicism and forming their own theologies. Is this any way to develop a path to God?

Another problem represented by current theologies is that they place their emphasis on dead images. I am well aware of expressions such as the "living Christ" or the "living Buddha," but these souls crossed into spirit from their physical bodies thousands of years ago.

These images of the past tend to be distorted with succeeding generations of Church hierarchies. The English poet William Blake described a Hall of Los, in which events in our lives are portrayed in the form of statues. It is only the focus of our attention on these figures that gives them life.

Quantum physics 200 years later demonstrates that our mind creates reality. Blake's depiction of the Akashic records is important because by accessing them we can learn more about our past errors, and view our potential futures to avoid repeating the same errors.

But just focusing on dead images alone is not going to lead you to God. True spiritual seekers want a live image to focus on. This is not a vision or an imaginary depiction. Seeing reality for what it is through spiritual eyes is my definition of a live image.

This viewing the forces that currently exist and are all around us is far more important than looking into the past and future. To truly have reality in our lives requires a knowing and understanding of these undercurrents, and a clear view of the path to God.

You can imagine the obstacles I face with patients who are

familiar with my work with past life regression and future life progression hypnotherapy. It is difficult to at first get the point across that these techniques are mere stepping stones to accessing the Higher Self.

OBEs have a deeper value than just relaxation and soul travel. They simulate what will actually occur following the death of the physical body. This is why I devote an entire section in Chapter 13 to training you with these exercises.

The illusions of the physical world must be recognized for what they are. A decision has to be made concerning the accuracy of what our mind records on a daily basis. By leaving our body and accessing our Higher Self, we can separate the karmic milk from the karmic curd. This contrast between the material world and our personal cosmic universe is one path to God.

To be assured that you are on a path to God, a certain amount of faith and confidence in this system needs to be established. We must make our own decisions, have faith in their correctness and absolutely know that they are right. This is spiritual empowerment.

We are not totally disavowing our human nature and basic personality by this process, merely modifying it and opening our consciousness to a higher power. You do not need to quit your job, divorce your spouse or run away from home to enter this path to God. Just look within and grow spiritually.

Karma is another major obstacle in our path to God. The Tibetans speak of a chain of originations. This refers to the concept that once an initial cause is created, the effects are repeated from lifetime to lifetime into many future incarnations.

When I guide you in Chapter 13 to the astral, causal, mental and etheric planes, you will be exposed to various temples of wisdom where your entrance to the path to God will be greatly facilitated. Your spirit guides and Higher Self will always be there to assist your growth and spiritual unfoldment.

The ascension/state of Grace technique is the last exercise I present. It is designed to train you to recreate what will occur when you are ready to graduate from the karmic cycle and enter the ascension path to God. Always bear in mind that no soul can rise above its own frequency vibrational rate and enter into the higher planes on its path to God until it is perfect, and freed of all karma.

During our OBEs, which also occur nightly as we dream, our soul is functioning in these other planes, or at least the Astral plane.[1] At the same time during our waking state we live in a physical body in the material world. We are able to function on both of these dimensions, but we must recognize the illusions of the physical plane and rise above all Earth distractions to place our self on the path to God.

In discovering our individual path to God we must keep in mind that the universe functions on very basic principles. Occasionally some spiritually evolved souls discovered samples of these principles. Their attempt to disseminate these laws to the world resulted in a distortion and padding of these paradigms by less enlightened individuals who followed them.

Buddha outlined eight clear steps to self-realization, but Buddhism became one of the most elaborately ritualized religions the world has ever seen, and the simple teaching was

---

[1] B. Goldberg, "Astral Voyages," op cit.

almost forgotten in the process. Moses presented ten commandments to the Hebrews, and an immensely complicated religion was the result. Jesus tried to simplify complex Jewish law and remove unnecessary rituals and hypocrisy, and the vast, worldwide complex of Christianity grew out of it. Mohammed channeled the Koran and developed a simple and straightforward religion based on the acknowledgement of God and five prayers a day, but to that was added the highly detailed codification of Islamic law.

Every religion professed to hold the secret teachings that emanated from God. Lao Tse presented his philosophy in language so simple that it was interpreted in many ways. Patanjali presented his secret teachings of Yoga to the East Indians. Bodhidharma reportedly brought the secret teachings of Buddha into China. The school he developed was Ch'an Buddhism, which later became Zen Buddhism in Japan.

Other examples of these secret teachings include the Sufis, the Old Testament and the New Testament. The early Christian writers of the Gospels made it clear that the outer meaning of what they wrote was not the whole of what they had to say. Several times Jesus states that he will explain to the disciples in secret the meaning of the parables, and he informs the crowds that his meaning will be clear only to those able to understand. Secret teachings are alleged to be hidden in Tibetan monasteries, the Sphinx in Egypt and in the writings of secret societies, such as the Rosicrucians. All of these organizations claim to possess the ultimate truth.

It is difficult to describe the workings of a path to God. We must forego all that we have been exposed to by society and start fresh. This is not easy to do, which is why the path to

God is always arduous. When on this path, the goal of seeking God seems to disappear and is replaced by an attainment of the next level, with the goal of going still further in spiritual unfoldment.

The state of nonactivity is used to describe this quest for beyond-the-next stage of God-realization. Soul liberation is achieved by the practice of nonactivity. This state can best be described as one in which we are sitting still and doing something leading to our spiritual growth.

I have designed the exercises presented in this book to assist you in creating your own state of nonactivity. Here you are receptive to a deliverance into the true realm of the higher planes and a development of inner wisdom of the God consciousness.

Part of this wisdom entails recognizing the illusions or maya of the physical plane. When we realize that it is all a game, the game of life can lead to the game of ascension if properly played. This is the challenge of the transitee in the *Tibetan Book of the Dead*. The voyaging soul of the departed is tested to recognize the illusions of the peaceful and wrathful Buddhas, which are merely the good and evil components of his own mind.

The Tibetan voyager is shown the mirror of karma. Few pass these tests and escape the wheel of birth and death. The mirror of karma is available to us now. Just about everyone we meet, every situation we experience that gives us pleasure or pain are karmic carryovers from unpaid karmic debts.

If we can look at the workings of our mind with the same indifference we show toward the inner workings of our physical body, unless a medical problem surfaces, we will quickly grasp the concept that nothing viewed by our five senses is real.

Let us once and for all break the mirror of karma and move out of the bondage of the karmic cycle to the path to God. Only when we recognize that our true self, the soul and its Higher Self, the soul and its Higher Self counterpart, is the component of our being that requires liberation.

Chapter 12:
The Ultimate Challenge

*T*he ultimate challenge in our ascension path is the resistance to temptations that impede our soul's path to perfection. Questions concerning evil more commonly than not appear in discussions of this sort.

Evil can be defined as those forces, values and persons destructive to one's spiritual growth. Few people, due to their own ego, want to consider that evil is conscious. The challenge of evil must be acknowledged. We simply can't blame it on the universe, or some fallen angel.

All of life on the physical plane exists in polarities, or opposites. We have life and death, joy and despair and so on. The ancient Chinese purported the concept of Yin and Yang. Therefore, God must be part of this polarity.

For there to be God, some say a devil must exist. Isn't evil the opposite of the good represented by God? Are not good and evil just two sides of the same coin? There could be no light without darkness. Some would say that darkness should be accepted because the individual's shadowside must be embraced. Only then can the destructive, dark side of human beings be integrated into psychological wholeness.

Vajrayana is a form of Buddhist meditation. One of its rituals involves gazing into the face of absolute evil, and, in mortal embrace, to become that face, that embodiment of absolute evil. I have previously discussed the Tibetan Book of the Dead's sections describing the peaceful and wrathful Buddhas, with the recommendation to the voyaging soul to embrace the wrathful deity in an attempt to integrate this evil aspect of one's personality.

I disagree with the Easterners. Psychic empowerment would be better demonstrated by taking a stance against evil, not accepting it but confronting this force. One can look also to the great myths: St. George did not "accept" the dragon; Shiva did not "integrate" the demon of ignorance over which he danced; Archangel Michael did not "embrace" Lucifer; and Christ did not "become" Satan's temptations. Individuals need to stand, face and conquer—not embrace—those forces destructive to their spiritual advancement. This is part of our ultimate challenge.

The development of psychic gifts corresponds to our spiritual evolution, as I have discussed earlier. However, we must be wary of the challenge of following a false guru or prophet who is able to perform psychic tricks. Such acts as materializing a precious gem out of thin air is impressive to spiritually naive souls who cannot discriminate between the spiritual and psychic use of power.

Esoteric tradition holds that on each upward level of the spectrum of consciousness, "cosmic" power is more available and more potent. Through the ages ways to develop supernormal powers have been kept secret, so that those motivated by fear, greed, power, or evil will not misuse them. There were many members of these Mystery School religions that misused these psychic gifts.

I have nothing against psychic development. In fact, my

practice is to encourage it. The only way to master these psychic powers is to tap into a higher power. The challenge again is to resist the misuse of these abilities.

We must recognize the responsibility that goes along with psychic development. In my book *Protected by the Light*,[1] I point out many instances of misuse of magic techniques that resulted in severe consequences for the malicious practitioner.

Even the well-meaning healing application of Wicca requires the permission of the ill persons before you can ethically send them light and love. We must always resist the temptation to use the mystic powers within us for negative purposes. Let us learn from the ancient shaman, priest and initiate of the sacred fire to pass the tests that make up the ultimate challenge.

The lower five planes were created by God as a training ground for our soul to gather knowledge, wisdom, love and other qualities to evolve spiritually. When we have passed these tests our reward is ascension into the higher planes to eventually join God.

If you believe in the devil or some other evil force, you must acknowledge that this antagonist to our growth creates traps, false signs and barriers to our spiritual unfoldment.

Theosophy talks about Lords of Karma, or Lipika, that have a vested interest in keeping souls with the karmic cycle. Apparently they cannot ascend, so if we all rise into the higher planes these Lipika would have no one to play with.

Whatever the mechanism, Lipika, the devil or simply spiritually evolved entities who are beyond us in development

---

[1] B. Goldberg, "Protected by the Light," op cit.

but still not happy campers, challenges are placed before us to test our spiritual muscle. The tests can manifest as attachment to earthly desires, public opinion, false happiness, vanity and so on.

This ritual of fire or trial is part of our world whether we like it or not. The spiritual exercises I present throughout this book are designed to guide you in passing these tests and properly facing the ultimate challenge.

When we reject people because they are different in their interests, appearance or philosophy, we are failing these spiritual tests. This is where public opinion comes into play. Do we not see this in schools, offices and churches? Being different subjects one to ridicule and sometimes ostracism. The tests of tolerance and forgiveness failed.

The forces in our world that feed into our insecurities become part of this ultimate challenge. Any expression of egotism, such as pride and vanity, feed into this vicious cycle of defense mechanism mentality. The distortion of our perception of the world, coupled with letting day-to-day circumstances distract you from your spiritual path, function to add to our challenges.

Awareness is one way to successfully meet the ultimate challenge. Awareness is consciousness, and until we come to recognize it within ourselves, we will never attain spiritual perfection. This awareness is far more than thought. It is an opening of our inner consciousness to our Higher Self.

Another challenge we face is separation. We must separate the physical from the emotional and the emotional from thought. Finally, separating thought from consciousness is necessary. Thought responds to the illusions of the physical plane, whereas consciousness is pure soul and leads us to the truth.

By concentrating our focus within we enter into a state of consciousness that detaches us from the material world. This opens up our inner awareness. We should never express an ambition to attain God-realization, since this is a negative principle.

Politicians express ambition to get elected and business people use ambition to get ahead at any cost. When concerning ourselves with God-realization, we should never apply such disrespectful and materialistic objectives.

The conscious mind plays many tricks during our quest for ascension. It is easily used by negative forces to instill fear and other negative emotions that make it impossible to progress spiritually. Our conscious mind is dominated by its own passions and harassed by its own desires.

Consciousness is an unmanifested force that has no being and performs no function. It just is, and as such represents the ultimate reality of all things. By perfecting our consciousness we prepare it to meet the ultimate challenge and ascend into the higher planes.

As you travel to other planes by way of your consciousness you develop your awareness. The farther we travel in spirit, the greater our awareness is. Recognizing its existence in each of us means we have passed the initial phase of the ultimate challenge.

Some refer to this lower form of consciousness as love; love binds life and all things together in an adhesiveness that cannot be broken as long as this love exists. When it is transformed to indifference or hatred these bonds are broken.

Because of its impermanence, I refer to love as a lower form of consciousness.

Our soul is the true essence of our being. All consciousness resides in our soul. Below the soul, everything, including all mental processes, represents illusions of the physical plane. This consciousness by way of the soul is the channel for God.

Outside of the soul lies the world of karma on the lower planes. Each of us must pay our own karmic debts and enter the path to God. Each of us also has the capability to detach ourselves from the physical body and voyage to all regions of the spiritual universe.

Other components of this ultimate challenge are the physical senses. These five senses create desire, which attempts to trap us in the lower worlds. The mind can follow these nonspiritual desires and continue creating negative karma resulting in further entanglements in the wheel of birth and death.

We can think of God as the divine consciousness. Our soul can detect aspects of this when we raise our own level of consciousness. Certain lights and sounds are detected when we acquire advance levels of spiritual growth and consciousness expansion. The God energy uses these lights and sounds to prepare us for our eventual ascension.

Consciousness Evolution and Meeting the Ultimate Challenge

Our consciousness evolves if we properly access our Higher Self. This results in an advanced form of spiritual empowerment and enlightenment. As our souls evolve, so does society, the sciences, the arts and civilization as a whole.

To assure our meeting the ultimate challenge, we need to include esoteric traditions to our development. This is the purpose of the spiritual exercises included in this book.

We need to develop our own special tradition for spiritual growth and enlightenment. This paradigm should fit in with our culture, our goals and our time. This mechanism must lead us toward a path of ascension in the near future, not trap us in repeating mistakes of the past.

If society objects to these traditions, then it is our responsibility to change our culture to pave the way for the ascension not just of ourselves individually, but of humankind as a whole.

With this in mind, I would like to present ten goals for your consideration that upon completion will facilitate your successfully meeting your ultimate challenge:

1.   To look within our Higher Self for our primary source of growth, creativity and enlightenment. By referring to our Higher Self for counsel, we are tapping into God's energy. The source of all enlightenment dwells within us. There is no more important approach we can take to meet our ultimate challenge than acknowledging the Higher Self, the God within, as the gateway to our ascension.

2.   To link the subconscious with the Higher Self, producing a spiritualized soul capable of responding to the forces and qualities of spirit. We need to focus our responsibility on preparing our soul to function as a representative of God. Worshiping God alone is not going to open the path to ascension. Our duty is to

achieve and maintain an illuminated mind and purified spirit.

1. To integrate the life of spirit through the enlightened activities of the personality on the physical plane. We can learn to bring heaven to Earth by tapping into the divine qualities of love and wisdom within our Higher Self and incorporate these in our life in the material world.

2. To learn and use the skills of understanding, devotion, patience, charity and so on to link the personality with all aspects of the Divine. By shaping our ethical behavior and self-expression to follow the dictates of our Higher Self, this divine manifestation in our physical plane life will be instituted.

3. To purify all aspects of our personality and soul so they become agents of God's energy. This entails actively participating in the life and work of God. By placing greater emphasis on purifying and preparing our very being to transmit spiritual forces without distortion, we increase our effectiveness in translating the life of God into a constructive self-expression.

4. To cultivate our psychic empowerment by linking our soul with the wisdom of its Higher Self. We must learn to discern truth and wisdom for ourselves and divest our natural tendency to exhibit co-dependent behavior. This psychic empowerment allows us to see through illusions, dogma, self-deception and attachments to the material plane.

5. To nurture an awareness of the underlying unity in the divine presence and our soul, and this ongoing

realization that we have our spiritual roots in God's heavenly domain. The ability to experience the presence of God through our Higher Self and our dealings with other human beings is paramount in establishing the kingdom of heaven on Earth.

6.   To recognize that it is our responsibility to spiritually develop our soul daily. We can integrate divine life into our conscious activities, attitudes and thoughts, and become a channel of divine force in encouraging humanity to greater heights of spiritual growth.

7.   To become consciously aware of the plan for the spiritual evolution of humanity and the role of spirit guides and our Higher Self. There is a group of ascended Masters, or enlightened beings, that guide and inspire human development and consciousness. It is important to learn how to participate in this divine plan and assist in its implementation.

8.   To ascend. This is the main purpose of our being on the physical plane. By applying the principles and exercises presented in this book, this will be attained. As unfathomable as it may be to many, we can all ascend by following simple principles and looking within to our Higher Self.

The more we remain attached to the material world, the more we impose limitations to our spiritual growth. Everything about our five senses and physical body has limitations. Our ears can detect only certain ranges of sounds. Each of our senses has specified physical limitations.

The faculties of the soul are endless. This is why we can

perfect this energy level. It has no limits. Once we dwell in soul consciousness, we are capable of seeing and knowing all things. Our awareness opens up to the divine Higher Self within us.

In Chapter 5, I discussed the different sounds associated with each plane. These sounds emanate from the higher planes. In a certain way they are the sounds of God. To appreciate these sounds we must be in the appropriate level of awareness to receive them. This awareness requires an increase in the frequency vibrational rate of our soul, or simply stated, a raise in consciousness.

The ultimate challenge is to overcome all the limiting factors present on the lower worlds. This especially applies to the illusions that so dominate the physical plane. When we pass the ultimate challenge, we are ready to ascend.

Chapter 13

Hypnotize Your Way to

Nirvana

_I_n this chapter we will discuss the use of hypnosis on preparing the soul for ascension. Many exercises will be presented to effect this goal. I will also discuss the advantages of OBEs, and how they can facilitate our spiritual unfoldment and prepare us for ascension itself.

Before I present various self-hypnosis exercises, a thorough discussion on the nature of our subconscious is necessary. The subconscious mind or soul is electromagnetic radiation and is equivalent to a radio or television signal. It is the energy that constitutes our true essence and must be purified before we can ascend.

Our subconscious mind's primary function is memory. It exerts a significant control over the functioning of our physical body in coordination with the conscious mind proper, or ego. Our subconscious is the source of all our behavior, including habits, phobias, and emotions.

The means by which the conscious mind perceives experiences and acts upon them originates from our subconscious. This mind is the receiver and transmitter of all psychic phenomena. Its main purpose is spiritual growth.

The one problem with the subconscious is that it obeys orders, and is very susceptible to what is fed into its memory banks by the analytical conscious mind, or willpower (ego), that receives its data from our five senses. Cynical and negative programming of our subconscious by the ego results in the neuroses that most of us exhibit.

All of our body's organ systems and functions are directly controlled by the subconscious. We do have DNA mechanically directing the replacement of our cells, but the daily supervision of our life processes falls under the direction of the subconscious.

Our behavior is also influenced by environmental factors and social experiences, in addition to conscious (ego) decisions. The operation of our body and the growth of our soul is influenced directly by the way we think and feel. Psychosomatic and energy medicine has corroborated this fact.

Fear is always the major block to our soul's growth. Since fear is an emotional response, we must understand that there are four primary effects we experience from an emotional level. These are fear (withdrawal), joy (expansion), action (physical or mental activity) and anger (attack).

Fear and/or anger combinations produce depression by directing this anger inward. The subconscious stores these memories as associations and these remain a part of our behavior unless changed by conscious or superconscious intervention. The conscious mind (ego) has no incentive to remove a stored association, as its purpose appears to be to prevent growth and keep "business as usual."

Our habits and negative tendencies ("self-defeating sequences") remain intact as long as they serve some useful purpose from the standpoint of the subconscious. Even if a habit is consciously undesirable, it remains in our behavior until reprogrammed out of the subconscious mind's memory bank and computer library.

Conventionally, this requires conscious attention and offers the subconscious a viable alternative to remove a bad habit. We will shortly see how the superconscious mind tap can accelerate this process. We see symptom substitution with conventional approaches, but not with superconscious mind taps. We must deal with all our habits, phobias, procrastinations and other self-defeating sequences if we are to perfect our soul.

Paranormal Sense Development

As we spiritually evolve, an increase in our psychic abilities is observed. Some examples of these gifts are: telepathy (the ability to read the thoughts of others), clairvoyance (seeing things that are occurring now but beyond the range of normal sight), clairaudience (hearing sounds that are currently being produced, but beyond the normal sense of hearing) and precognition (the ability to perceive events in the future). Hypnosis can speed up this psychic development.

Hypnotic Spiritual Fulfillment

Through hypnosis we will learn to improve our awareness, skills, self-image, happiness and creativity. This amounts to an increase in our growth at all levels, especially spiritually.

It is only fear-producing beliefs that interfere with our soul's natural progress toward spiritual growth. Self-hypnosis will urge us toward discovering better and better ways of doing things physically, mentally, socially and spiritually.

Archeologists and anthropologists have demonstrated that even the earliest humans developed skills in art, crafts and inventing in the midst of harsh environments and constant danger by predators and food shortage. Their curiosity was most likely stimulated by their Higher Self, as we have records of hypnosis and OBE techniques being practiced over 15,000 years ago.[1]

Conscious Awareness

Directing our attention and awareness in response to experience or thoughts is the only capability our conscious mind has in affecting our behavior. We use the term free will to describe this choice and subsequent action.

This free will is not the freedom to do anything we want whenever or however we want, nor to make anything happen when we want it to, nor to make others do what we want them to do. Even though we can learn techniques to increase our effectiveness, we can't make someone like us by exerting our will. We can't make ourselves or the world perfect just by "willing" it (which really means "wishing hard"). What we can do, however, is to choose or decide how we are going to respond to our experience of life, what we are going to do from this moment forward and in any future moment to change either ourselves or the circumstances. At any moment of conscious awareness we have that freedom to choose.

The subconscious accesses the Higher Self or super-conscious, and receives both direction and inspiration from its perfect counterpart. If no data are received from the Higher

---

[1] B. Goldberg, "Astral Voyages," op cit.

Self, the subconscious will allow the conscious mind to program it as to what to do. This is rarely beneficial, as the conscious mind or ego tries to resist change or growth of any type.

Our subconscious is continually receiving data in the form of our five senses, feelings, imagery and thoughts. It then stores this data into its memory banks and directs the conscious mind how to act on this directive. Often these impressions are stimulated by outside events and are not necessarily part of our ordinary or even habitual thinking. Whatever our conscious reaction to these presentations is, our subconscious takes that as a directive to initiate a direct order.

Since the subconscious is our soul, it does contain, or have access to via the Akashic records, information about all of our past, present, parallel and future lives. It also receives communication from the Higher Self. The subconscious will bring any aspect of this stored data to our awareness, whether or not we are cognizant of this process, for the conscious mind to analyze and take action.

It is more difficult to alter habitual thinking patterns than it is to change physical manifestations of these habits. Without accessing the Higher Self, the only way to alter the habitual thinking of the subconscious is to consciously keep the desired pattern in the forefront of one's mind until the subconscious has accepted it as a new habit. This is the method behind the success of positive thinking affirmations, and conventional hypnotherapy.

The subconscious is very susceptible to repeated suggestion, but if the reprogramming is not complete, the subconscious will revert to its old habits once the repetition has ceased. Our subconscious will go on doing a thing in a certain way until one takes the time to teach it otherwise, or until it learns from someone else (our Higher Self) without our knowledge.

Cleansing

Our subconscious actually functions as an energy distributor, or agent, of the Higher Self. The subconscious is not the true source of our origin from the God energy that is represented by the Higher Self. It is our subconscious that does determine how much power or energy we have available at any given time. Our potential energy is infinite, and this effective energy is limited only by our subconscious beliefs and habits. To increase our effective energy and power, we have to find some way of changing or overcoming any limitations we may have established.

Everything in this world is accomplished by the transformation of one kind of energy into another.

The term "cleansing" is used by me to refer to the introduction of the subconscious to the superconscious or Higher Self. When this state is achieved, the patient's subconscious energy level, or frequency vibrational rate, will be raised since it is now exposed to the perfect level as represented by the superconscious.

The REM (dream) cycle at night is when this cleansing is most effective. The reason for this is that none of our defense mechanisms are functioning while we enter any part of the sleep cycle. This is equivalent to walking down a football field that is devoid of defense players. As long as you don't drop the ball, you will score a touchdown every time.

These defense mechanisms are the only real obstacle to our growth or healing. The REM cycle offers us the ideal opportunity to use this hypnotic introduction of our subconscious to its perfect counterpart (superconscious) to effect this raising of the quality of the subconscious energy level.

Another effect of this mechanism is an increase in the immune system of our physical body against disease, and our emotional component against mood swings. The energy of our superconscious raises that of our subconscious. This now moves on to the emotions, which correspondingly affects the physical.

Figure 5 illustrates this concept. You will note that the arrows always move from the energy level down to the physical. We can avoid the emotional component in the case of pain.

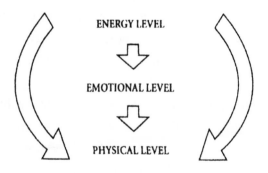

The dream state, with its deep level of natural hypnosis and its lack of defense mechanisms, affords us the perfect opportunity to truly dream our problems away.

Back in 1977 when I developed the cleansing technique, I named it the superconscious mind tap. One reason why this method is so effective is that the soul's energy can never be lowered, but it can be raised. Conducting a superconscious mind tap (or "cleansing") is the most effective method I know of to boost the energy of the subconscious. Clinically this will be observed as an increase in self-image, motivation, energy and the expression of a success-type personality.

Ninety-eight percent of our energy cleansing takes place during the REM cycle. There is nothing to prevent our soul's energy from raising its quality. There is no other time during the day when this situation exists. Normally our REM cycle conducts a type of emotional cleansing, which is necessary for life preservation.

Energy cleansing does not happen automatically, since it is not required to preserve life. We use about one of our three hours in REM for energy cleansing, if properly trained. Since each minute in hypnosis is equivalent to three or four Earth minutes, three to four hours of therapeutic energy cleansing is actually experienced by the individual. It is no wonder that this therapy is so short, successful and popular.

The reason this energy cleansing does not simply occur every night during our REM cycle is that it is not essential for life. Emotional cleansing must take place if we are to maintain our vital functions and physical life. Since Nature is only concerned about life preservation and not spiritual growth, the latter must be specially directed.

I have presented the script of the superconscious mind tap in Chapter 4. My main point in this discussion is that it is not necessary to understand why an issue originated, or in what past/future life the condition began. As long as you are motivated and can access your Higher Self, soul healing will take place and your subconscious mind's energy level will be raised.

Here are some applications of the superconscious mind tap:

1.   Receiving spiritual guidance from your Higher Self or Masters and Guides.
2.   Scanning past lives, the future of your current lifetime, and future lifetimes.
3.   Contacting departed loved ones.
4.   Removing attached entities.
5.   Spiritual protection from negative projection techniques.
6.   Contacting the souls of unborn children.
7.   Raising your soul's energy in preparation for ascension.[2]

The cleansing mechanism being manifested during our dream cycle is an important process in our goal toward ascension. Even Shakespeare alluded to this paradigm when he wrote:

> To sleep! perchance to dream
> ay, there's the rub;
> For in that sleep of death
> what dreams may come,

---

[2] B. Goldberg, "Soul Healing," op cit.

When we have shuffled off
this mortal coil,
Must give us pause.[3]

This "mortal coil" affects the amount of time and energy required by each of us to sever ourselves from the cycle of birth and death and finally ascend.

Your Hypnotic Setting

Before I present self-hypnotic exercises, a comment or two on the room you use to practice is in order. Select a room that is free of audio, visual and odor distractions. The temperature of this room should be a few degrees above room temperature.

Lying in a recliner is the best position to be in for self-hypnosis. You are less likely to fall asleep in this type of chair, as compared to a bed or couch. Music playing in the background is also highly recommended.

I suggest you keep a blanket and a cassette player by your recliner if you want to record your experiences or simply play relaxing music tapes during your session. Headphones help deepen the hypnotic trance, as well as block out extraneous sounds. My book *New Age Hypnosis*[4] teaches you how to make your own tapes.

Spiritual Protection

I include a white light protection technique on my scripts for self-hypnosis. If you refer back to the superconscious mind tap script given in Chapter 4, you will note its presence. In

---

[3] Hamlet, 3.1.65-68.
[4] B. Goldberg, "New Age Hypnosis" (St. Paul: Llewellyn, 1998).

order to effectively apply this method some visualization is necessary.

The art of visualization involves producing images in your mind. By relaxing the body and setting aside the conscious mind, we can enhance our ability to create mental images. It is not necessary to see these images in detail for this method to work. Trying too hard will only act as an obstacle in your quest to use visual imagery.

Here is a detailed spiritual protection technique that trains you in visual imagery, as well as provides a powerful form of spiritual protection to your soul.

1. Sit comfortably or lie down with your shoes off and dressed in loosely fitting clothes. Breathe deeply for two minutes.

2. Breathe in deeply and as you exhale, visualize a circle of energy in the form of a white light above your head. Sense this energy moving in a clockwise direction as it moves down your body.

3. This circle of white light now takes the shape of a funnel and appears in a corkscrew as it slowly descends down your body. See certain fragments of negative energy being ejected from your aura as it makes its descent.

4. Imagine this energy field finally moving into your feet. Now see a gold band of energy moving up from your feet to your head. As this gold band rises, it leaves a thin gold shield around your aura. This is a protective covering that only allows positive energy to enter your auric field.

5.   Spend five minutes with this last visualization. Now take a few deep breaths and relax.

A Basic Self-hypnosis Exercise

The following script will train you to enter into (not under) a self-hypnotic trance state and relax your body: As I suggest you concentrate on a certain muscle group, imagine a warm and relaxing feeling permeating each and every fiber of this muscle group. This will serve to facilitate both the relaxation of these muscles and your depth of self-hypnosis.

Begin with the forehead. Loosen the muscles in your forehead. Now your eyes. Loosen the muscles around your eyes. Your eyelids relax. Now your face, your face relaxes. And your mouth . . . relax the muscles around your mouth, and even the inside of your mouth. Your chin; let it sag and feel heavy. And as you relax your muscles, your breathing continues r-e-g-u-l-a-r-l-y and d-e-e-p-l-y, deeply within yourself. Now your neck, your neck relaxes. Every muscle, every fiber in your neck relaxes. Your shoulders relax . . . your arms . . . your elbows . . . your forearms . . . your wrists . . . your hands . . . and your fingers relax. Your arms feel loose and limp; heavy and loose and limp. Your whole body begins to feel loose and limp. Your neck muscles relax; the front of your neck; the back muscles. Keep breathing deeply and relax Now your chest. The front part of your chest relaxes and the back part of your chest relaxes. Your abdomen . . . the pit of your stomach, that relaxes. The small of your back, loosen the muscles. Your hips . . . your thighs . . . your knees relax . . . even the muscles in your legs. Your ankles . . . your feet . . . and your toes. Your whole body feels loose and limp. And now as you feel the muscles relaxing, you will notice that you begin to feel heavy

and relaxed and tired all over. Your body begins to feel v-e-r-y, v-e-r-y tired and you are going to feel d-r-o-w-s-i-e-r and d-r-o-w-s-i-e-r, from the top of your head right down to your toes. Every breath you take is going to deepen this trance. Deeper and deeper and deeper relaxed. You feel your body getting drowsier and drowsier.

Alright now. Sleep now and rest. You did very well. Listen very carefully. I'm going to count forward now from 1 to 5. When I reach the count of 5 you will be able to remember everything you experienced and re-experienced, you'll feel very relaxed, refreshed, you'll be able to do whatever you have planned for the rest of the day or evening. You'll feel very positive about what you've just experienced and very motivated about your confidence and ability to play this tape again to experience self-hypnosis. Alright now. 1 very very deep, 2 you're getting a little bit lighter, 3 you're getting much much lighter, 4 very very light, 5 awaken. Wide awake and refreshed.

Interdimensional Travel

In this section we will discuss and present techniques of leaving the body to travel to the other dimensions that I described in Chapter 5. To truly experience the liberation of the confines of the physical body, we must learn to master OBEs.

Ascension is an out-of-body state, as are all dreams and many forms of deep meditation and hypnosis. The well-publicized near-death experiences (NDEs) you are probably familiar with are a type of OBE. Fortunately, we don't have to clinically die to experience this out-of-body phenomenon. These OBE techniques are all perfectly safe. I have conducted thousands of these with my patients, and have personally

traveled out of my body to these other planes. The only real
danger is in not mastering these approaches and inhibiting your
spiritual growth.

Interdimensional travel has been called many other names.
Some of these are:

> Astral projection
> Traveling clairvoyance
> Remote viewing
> Out-of-body experience
> Near-death experience

Often my patients describe leaving their body as a "state
of ecstasy," or "beside oneself with joy." Most people want to
have this experience over and over again.

The following represent characteristics of interdimensional
travel:

- The senses of perception are more acute in this new
  dimension.
- The astral body is weightless, but possesses very acute
  perceptive abilities, especially toward bright and vivid
  colors and sounds.
- The physical body becomes immobile and rigid (this
  effect can be neutralized by white light protection and
  other techniques I incorporate in my tapes). The
  voyager is unable to move his or her limbs. This
  response ends once the two bodies separate.
- It is the physical body now that appears as an empty
  shell. The focal point of consciousness is from the
  astral body.
- Voyagers commonly describe moving through a dark

tunnel and entering a white light.

- Awareness of being out-of-the body is usually due to the inability to move objects on the physical plane.
- We perceive some portion of some environment that could not possibly be perceived from where our physical body is known to be at the time.
- We know at the time that we are not dreaming or experiencing a fantasy. Although we may deduce that this cannot be happening, we are in possession of all our critical functions and later can state with absolute certainty that the astral voyage was not a dream.
- A pulsating silver cord connects the astral body to the physical body. This cord appears to become thinner as the distance between the two bodies increases.
- The soul commonly leaves the physical body at the solar plexus or stomach area, for those individuals who are relatively novice at astral voyaging. When you become more adept at leaving the body, other exit points are:
  v The third-eye region between the eyebrows
  v The back of the head
  v The heart chakra
  v The seventh chakra, located at the top of the head
- The presence of spirit guides, other departed souls and fellow astral voyagers are reported.
- Some astral voyagers remain in the same location with the physical body, while others travel thousands of miles away.
- When beyond the physical body, there are no physical laws as we know on the Earth plane. All time is

simultaneous, so that you can view any past, present or
future activity on the physical plane.

- Distances are traveled at the speed of light. All the
  astral body has to do is think of a location (when
  properly trained) and the body arrives there in an
  instant.
- Feelings of "tuggings" at the back of the head are felt
  when the OBE is too long in duration. This precedes
  the return to the physical body.
- Fear that the unattended physical body will die is the
  most common trigger for the astral body to reunite with
  its physical counterpart. A loud noise can also bring
  about the end of this metaphysical sojourn. This final
  step occurs in an instant.

It is important to note that throughout any form of
interdimensional travel you will always be both assisted and
protected by your Higher Self. Nothing can prevent you from
returning to your physical body. Every one of us can and does
experience this state while we dream, for example. These
techniques are designed for the novice, as well as the
experienced astral voyager.

Advantages of Voyaging to Other Planes

The elimination of the fear of death, and freedom from all
physical, mental, emotional, psychic and spiritual entanglements are just some of the many advantages to traveling to
these other dimensions. We must not neglect to consider the
attainment of love and wisdom as benefits from these
experiences.

Regardless of our motives for dimensional travel, by transcending the physical body we are exposed to spiritual knowledge and growth far beyond what we normally receive on the physical plane.

Preparing to Leave the Body

A change in our state of consciousness is necessary in order for us to voyage beyond the physical plane. Although we can occasionally bring about an OBE solely through the concentrated effort of willpower, the conditions that are most favorable to astral voyaging are just prior to falling asleep and times of utter stillness.

Always bear in mind that we all possess the capability of leaving the physical body, and do so every night when we dream. The path traveled by our astral body during its projection is one of becoming disengaged from our physical body and floating slightly above it. Next it rises horizontally, moving somewhat in front of the physical body and becoming upright. This process is reversed when the astral body returns to the physical and reunites with it.

I highly recommend that your physical body remain motionless during our OBE. Any purposeful movement can result in an early termination of your interdimensional voyage. To return to the physical body at any time is really quite simple. Just focus your concentration on moving a part of your physical body (blinking your eye, twitching a finger, etc.) and you will immediately reunite with your physical counterpart.

Your initial voyages will most likely be to the astral plane. There is a buffer zone that separates the physical plane from its astral counterpart. Many describe this region as an underground silo approximately 200 feet in diameter and about 2,000 feet deep.

The ceiling of this silo appears as a canopy of white light and looks like a sky filled with specks of twinkling stars. Other voyagers report a pastoral scene or being on a mountaintop between the two dimensions.

A Hypnotic OBE Exercise

With this added background you are now ready for your initial OBEs. Try this simple hypnotic exercise in a quiet and comfortable practice room.

Let yourself relax completely...and breathe quickly ... in...and out. And as you do so you will gradually sink into a deeper, deeper sleep. And as you sink into this deeper, deeper sleep, I want you to concentrate on the sensations you can feel in your left hand and arm. You will feel that your left hand is gradually becoming lighter and lighter. It feels just as though your wrists were tied to a balloon...as if it were gradually pulled up...higher and higher...away from the chair.

It wants to rise up...into the air...toward the ceiling. Let it rise...higher and higher. Just like a cork...floating on water. And, as it floats up...into the air...your whole body feels more and more relaxed...heavier and heavier...and you are slowing sinking into a deeper, deeper sleep.

Your left hand feels even lighter and lighter. Rising up into the air...as if it were being pulled up toward the ceiling. Lighter and lighter...light as a feather. Breathe deeply...and let yourself relax completely. And as your hand gets lighter and lighter...and rises higher and higher into the air...your body is feeling heavier and heavier...and you are falling into a deep, deep sleep.

Now your whole arm, from the shoulder to the wrist,is becoming lighter and lighter. It is leaving the chair...and floating upwards...into the air.

Up it comes...into the air,...higher and higher. Let it rise...higher and higher,...higher and higher. It is slowly floating up...into the air...and as it does so...you are falling into a deeper, deeper trance.

Visualize a floating sensation spreading throughout your entire body. Continue breathing deeply and feel your soul leaving your body through the top of your head, as it rises up beyond the Earth plane to the astral plane. Note the warm feeling now spreading and permeating throughout your entire body. Allow yourself to receive the guidance and love from your Higher Self and spirit guides.

Play New Age Music for 2 Minutes

Experience a feeling of total love and peace. Let yourself immerse your complete awareness in a sense of balance and centering of your soul's energy.

Play New Age Music for 4 Minutes

Alright now. Sleep now and rest. You did very well. Listen very carefully. I'm going to count forward now from 1 to 5. When I reach the count of 5 you will be back in the body, you will be able to remember everything you experienced and re-experienced, you'll feel very relaxed, refreshed, you'll be able to do whatever you have planned for the rest of the day or evening. You'll feel very positive about what you've just experienced and very motivated about your confidence and ability to play this tape again to experience leaving your physical body safely. Alright now. 1 very very deep, 2 you're getting a little bit lighter, 3 you're getting much much lighter, 4 very very light, 5 awaken. Wide awake and refreshed.

The following OBE hypnotic exercise incorporates a

number of different approaches and facilitates your own
spiritual growth:

Now listen very carefully. I want you to imagine a bright
white light coming down from above and entering the top of
your head, filling your entire body. See it, feel it and it
becomes reality. Now imagine an aura of pure white light
emanating from your heart region. Again surrounding your
entire body. Protecting you. See it, feel it and it becomes
reality. Now only your Masters and Guides and highly
evolved loving entities who mean you well will be able to
influence you during this or any other hypnotic session. You
are totally protected by this aura of pure white light.

Now focus in on how comfortable and relaxed you are,
free of distractions, free from physical and emotional obstacles
that prevent you from safely leaving and returning to the
physical body. You will perceive and remember all that you
encounter during this experience. You will recall in detail
when you are physically awake only these matters that will be
beneficial to your physical, mental and spiritual being and
experience. Now begin to sense the vibrations around you, and
in your own mind begin to shape and pull them into a ring
around your head. Do this for a few moments now.

Play New Age Music for 2 Minutes

Now as you begin to attract these vibrations into your
inner awareness, they begin to sweep throughout your body
making it rigid and immobile. You are always in complete
control of this experience. Do this now as you perceive
yourself rigid and immobile with these vibrations moving
along and throughout your entire body.

Play New Age Music for 3 Minutes

You have done very well. Pulse these vibrations. Perceive
yourself feeling the pulse of these vibrations throughout your
entire awareness. In your own mind's eye, reach out one of

your arms and grasp some object that you know is out of normal reach. Feel the object and let your astral hand pass through it. Your mind is using your astral arm, not your physical arm, to feel the object. As you do this you are becoming lighter and lighter and your astral body is beginning to rise up from your physical body. Do this now.

Play New Age Music for 3 Minutes

You've done very well. Now, using other parts of your astral body (your head, feet, chest and back) repeat this exercise and continue to feel lighter and lighter as your astral body begins to rise up from your physical body. Do this now.

Play New Age Music for 3 Minutes

Now think of yourself as becoming lighter and lighter throughout your body. Perceive yourself floating up as your entire astral body lifts up and floats away from your physical body. Concentrate on blackness and remove all fears during this process. Imagine a helium-filled balloon rising and pulling your astral body with it up and away from your physical body. Do this now.

Play New Age Music for 3 Minutes

Now orient yourself to this new experience. You are out of your body, relaxed, safe and totally protected by the white light. Concentrate on a place, not far away, that you would like to visit with your astral body. Now go to this place. Do this now. Perceive this new environment.

Play New Age Music for 3 Minutes

You've done very well. Now I want you to travel to a destination much farther away. It can be a location across the country or anywhere around the world. Take a few moments and think of this destination and you will be there in a few moments. Do this now.

Play New Age Music for 3 Minutes

Alright now. Sleep now and rest. You did very well. Listen very carefully. I'm going to count forward now from 1to 5. When I reach the count of 5 you will be back in the body, you will be able to remember everything you experienced and re-experienced, you'll feel very relaxed, refreshed, you'll be able to do whatever you had planned for the rest of the day or evening. You'll feel very positive about what you've just experienced and very motivated about your confidence and ability to play this tape again to experience leaving your physical body safely. Alright now. 1 very very deep, 2 you're getting a little bit lighter, 3 you're getting much much lighter, 4 very very light, 5 awaken. Wide awake and refreshed.

Here is another technique to leave the body that involves visual imagery:

Now listen very carefully. I want you to imagine a bright white light coming down from above and entering the top of your head. Filling your entire body. See it, feel it and it becomes reality. Now imagine an aura of pure white light emanating from your heart region. Again surrounding your entire body. Protecting you. See it, feel it and it becomes reality. Now only your Masters and Guides and highly evolved loving entities who mean you well will be able to influence you during this or any other hypnotic session. You are totally protected by this aura of pure white light.

You are about to embark on an imaginary journey, during which your awareness will be introduced to perceptions that are quite different from anything you have encountered before. You absolutely have the ability to voyage to the astral plane or beyond. Your silver cord will always remain attached to your physical body, protecting you and transmitting communication from your Higher Self to your subconscious.

Continued practice will ensure your success. Your voyages will only be to the upper astral plane or beyond. There is no possibility of ending up on the lower astral plane. Your Higher Self and Masters and Guides are always with you, advising and protecting you. Only positive entities will be a part of this experience.

Now raise your vibrations spreading throughout your body from the bottom of the spine to the top of the head. Feel the vibrations accentuate this ascension. Do this now.

Play New Age Music for 2 Minutes

Your astral body is now separating itself from the physical. See yourself in your mind's eye leave your body through the top of your head. See it happening in your mind and feel it happening in your body.

See your astral body float just about your physical body. As I count forward from 1 to 10, on the count of 10 you will arrive at your upper astral plane destination. 1, 2, 3, moving toward this plane. 4, 5, halfway there. 6, 7, 8, almost there. 9, 10, you are there.

Now begin exploring this dimension at your leisure. Record everything you see, hear, touch, taste and feel in your subconscious, to be remembered later. Do this now.

Play New Age Music for 3 Minutes

Now begin your trip back to the physical plane by first entering a brilliant white light you now see before you. Descend back to your room and merge with your physical body. Note the warm feeling now spreading and permeating throughout your entire body. Stay with this feeling for a few moments.

Experience a feeling of total love and peace. Let yourself

immerse your complete awareness in a sense of balance and centering of your soul's energy. Stay with this feeling for a few more moments.

Play New Age Music for 2 Minutes

Alright now. Sleep now and rest. You did very, very well. Listen very carefully. I'm going to count forward now from 1 to 5. When I reach the count of 5, you will be able to remember everything you experienced. You'll feel very relaxed, refreshed, and you'll be able to do whatever you have planned for the rest of the day or evening. You'll feel very positive about what you've just experienced and very motivated about your confidence and ability to play this tape again to voyage to other dimensions. Alright now. 1, very, very deep. 2, you're getting a little bit lighter. 3, you're getting much, much lighter. 4, very, very light. 5, awaken. Wide awake and refreshed.

It is often easiest to practice leaving the body just prior to falling asleep. Here is an exercise that uses this state of mind to facilitate traveling to another plane.

1.   Before going to sleep, keep a constant but vague awareness of your own identity. Then shift your focus from your body into blackness. Visualize a black inner screen with your eyes closed. This screen is pitch black.

2.   As you lie in bed focus your mind on relaxing your entire body. When this has been accomplished, pay particular attention to relaxing the muscles across both temples. This area extends from between the eyebrows to an inch above the ear (the "third eye").

3.   Listen for a faint high whistle at the top of your head, or any other sound that is not created by your physical

environment.

4.   Using suggestion, create a tingly sensation moving
        through this third eye region and flowing downward
        throughout your physical body. Magnify the sound and
        perceive it as a current of energy flowing from the
        eyebrows down the physical body to the feet and back
        to the forehead. This sound current of energy now
        creates a vibration that surrounds your physical
        body.

5.   Imagine your astral body vibrating out through the
        third-eye region of your head. You may instead project
        an image of your astral body separating from your
        physical body from the top of your head.

When you use this technique there are some considerations
you need to be aware of:

•   Don't become frustrated if you experience your mind
        wandering during this contemplation.
•   Remove any expectation of actually feeling your two
        bodies separating. More likely to occur is a shift in
        your awareness during the early stages of your first
        sleep cycle of being out-of-the-body.
•   Eliminate the tendency to expect a full OBE with this
        approach. Just relax and enjoy this experience.
        This next technique is a more advanced form of OBE,
        and should be practiced only after mastering the
        previous exercises presented:

Now listen very carefully. I want you to imagine a bright

white light coming down from above and entering the top of your head. Filling your entire body. See it, feel it and it becomes reality. Now imagine an aura of pure white light emanating from your heart region. Again surrounding your entire body. Protecting you. See it, feel it and it becomes reality. Now only your Masters and Guides and highly evolved loving entities who mean you well will be able to influence you during this or any other hypnotic session. You are totally protected by this aura of pure white light.

Now focus in on how comfortable and relaxed you are, free of distractions, free from physical and emotional obstacles that prevent you from safely leaving and returning to the physical body. You will perceive and remember all that you encounter during this experience. You will recall in detail when you are physically awake only these matters that will be beneficial to your physical and mental being and experience. Now begin to sense the vibrations around you and in your own mind begin to shape and pull them into a ring around your head. Do this for a few moments now.

Play New Age Music for 2 Minutes

Now as you begin to attract these vibrations into your inner awareness, they begin to sweep throughout your body, making it rigid and immobile. You are always in complete control of this experience. Do this now as you perceive yourself rigid and immobile with these vibrations moving along and throughout your entire body.

Play New Age Music for 3 Minutes

You have done very well. Pulse these vibrations. Perceive yourself feeling the pulse of these vibrations throughout your entire awareness.

Feel yourself now able to leave your physical body and travel safely and protected by the white light of your Higher Self to the astral, causal, mental or etheric plane. Your

Masters and Guides will also be there for you, assisting you in obtaining the greatest benefit from this experience.

And now going deeper and deeper and deeper, feeling your mind going deeply into trance, feeling your body going deeply into trance, your whole mind-body going deeper, and deeper, as you know and respond to a positive and spiritual force that is greater than any you have known or responded to before for this purpose of deepening trance.

And that force will continue to pull and to draw you, deeper and ever deeper, as now you are becoming very aware of your body, of the form and the substance of your body, and finding yourself now surrounded by darkness, and knowing that your soul's energy has been transported out from your physical body into another dimension.

Your soul is now voyaging to another dimension and taking you deeper and deeper into trance, and toward important new experiences, and liberating within what you have, but in the past could not use. And you will go deeper in order that you may become free.

As I count forward from 1 to 10 you will arrive on the count of 10 at a learning temple on either the astral, causal, mental or etheric plane. If you would like to select a particular plane to visit concentrate on that particular plane now.

Number 1, 2, 3 moving quickly toward this plane. 2, 3, 4, 5 you are halfway there. 6, 7, 8 almost there. 9 and 10 you are there. Take a few minutes and orient yourself to this learning temple. Now you may access your Akashic records and communicate with your Higher Self and/or spirit guides. You may ask any questions about your karmic purpose, past/future life ties with loved ones and anything else you would like to know. Do this now.

Play New Age Music for 3 Minutes

At this time you are free to explore this plane. I want you to take a tour of this dimension accompanied by your Higher Self and perhaps a spirit guide that will describe the components on this plane, and how this experience may assist you in your own spiritual growth. Do this now.

Play New Age Music for 3 Minutes

Alright now. Sleep now and rest. You did very very well. Listen very carefully. I'm going to count forward now from 1 to 5. When I reach the count of 5 you will be back in your physical body, you will be able to remember everything you experienced and re-experienced, you'll feel very relaxed, refreshed, you'll be able to do whatever you have planned for the rest of the day or evening. You'll feel very positive about what you've just experienced and very motivated about your confidence and ability to play this tape again to experience leaving your physical body safely. Alright now. 1 very very deep, 2 you're getting a little bit lighter, 3 you're getting much much lighter, 4 very very light, 5 awaken. Wide awake and refreshed.

Conscious Out-of-body Experience

In my book *Peaceful Transition*[5] I present in detail the concept of conscious dying. The basis of this approach is to merge with Higher Self at the precise moment of death. By successfully attaining this continuity of consciousness, we can perfect our soul and ascend.

Here is the script of the conscious out-of-body experience (OBE):

Now listen very carefully. I want you to imagine a bright white light coming down from above and entering the top of your head. Filling your entire body. See it, feel it and it becomes reality. Now imagine an aura of pure white light emanating

---

[5] B. Goldberg, "Peaceful Transition," op cit.

from your heart region. Again surrounding your entire body. Protecting you. See it, feel it, and it becomes reality. Now only your Masters and Guides Higher Self and highly evolved loving entities who mean well will be able to influence you during this or any other hypnotic session. You are totally protected by this aura of pure white light.

Now focus in on how comfortable and relaxed you are, free of distractions, free from physical and emotional obstacles that prevent you from safely leaving and returning to the physical body. You will perceive and remember all that you encounter during this experience. You will recall in detail when you are physically awake only these matters that will be beneficial to your physical and mental being and experience. Now begin to sense the vibrations around you, and in your own mind begin to shape and pull them into a ring around your head. Do this for a few moments now.

Play New Age Music for 2 Minutes

Now as you begin to attract these vibrations into your inner awareness, they begin to seep throughout your body making it rigid and immobile. You are always in complete control of this experience. Do this now as you perceive yourself rigid and immobile with these vibrations moving along and throughout your entire body.

Play New Age Music for 2 Minutes

You have done very well. Pulse these vibrations. Perceive yourself feeling the pulse of these vibrations throughout your entire awareness. In your own mind's eye, reach out one of your arms and grasp some object that you know is out of normal reach. Feel the object and let your astral hand pass through it. Your mind is using your astral arm, not your physical arm, to feel the object. As you do this you are becoming lighter and lighter and your astral body is beginning to rise up from your physical body. Do this now.

Play New Age Music for 2 Minutes

You've done very well. Now using other parts of your astral body (your head, feet, chest and back) repeat this exercise and continue to feel lighter and lighter as your astral body begins to rise up from your physical body. Do this now.

Play New Age Music for 2 Minutes

Now think of yourself as becoming lighter and lighter throughout your body. Perceive yourself floating up as your entire astral body lifts up and floats away from your physical body. Concentrate on blackness and remove all fears during this process. Imagine a helium-filled balloon rising and pulling your astral body with it up and away from your physical body. Do this now.

Play New Age Music for 2 Minutes

See how easy it is to leave the body while remaining in complete contact with your Higher Self. This is the process of conscious dying. It is that simple. Now ask your Higher Self for any instruction that will assist your spiritual growth. Remember, your Higher Self is all knowledgeable and has access to your Akashic records.

Now slowly and carefully state your desire for information or an experience and let your Higher Self work for you. Let it help you raise your soul's energy.

Play New Age Music for 3 Minutes

You have done very well. Now I want you to further open up the channels of communication by removing any obstacles and allowing yourself to receive information and experiences that will directly apply to and help better your present lifetime. Allow yourself to receive more advanced and more specific information from your Higher Self and Masters and Guides to raise your frequency and improve your karmic subcycle. Maintain the communication and connection with your Higher

Self. You are one with your Higher Self. This connection will always exist, even when the physical body dies. Allow your Higher Self to instruct you. Do this now.

Play New Age Music for 3 Minutes

Alright now. Sleep now and rest. You did very very well. Listen very carefully. I'm going to count forward now from 1 to 5. When I reach the count of 5 you will be back in your physical body. You will be able to remember everything you experienced and re-experienced, you'll feel very relaxed, refreshed, you'll be able to do whatever you have planned for the rest of the day or evening. You'll feel very positive about what you've just experienced and very motivated about your confidence and ability to play this tape again to experience conscious dying. Alright now. 1 very very deep, 2 you're getting a little bit lighter, 3 you're getting much much lighter, 4 very very light, 5 awaken. Wide awake and refreshed.

Soul Plane Ascension

The mechanism of ascension consists of perfecting the soul, rising to the soul plane and finally ascending into the higher planes. This exercise will allow you to experience the soul plane and to simulate the preliminary step to your eventual ascension:

Now listen very carefully. I want you to imagine a bright white light coming down from above and entering the top of your head. Filling your entire body. See it, feel it and it becomes reality. Now imagine an aura of pure white light emanating from your heart region. Again surrounding your entire body. Protecting you. See it, feel it and it becomes reality. Now only your Higher Self, Masters and Guides and highly evolved loving entities who mean you well will be able to influence you during this or any other hypnotic session. You are totally protected by this aura of pure white light.

In a few moments I am going to count from 1 to 20. As I do

so you will feel yourself rising up to the superconscious mind level where you will be able to receive information from your Higher Self and your Masters and Guides. Number 1 rising up. 2, 3, 4 rising higher. 5, 6, 7, letting information flow. 8, 9, 10, you are halfway there. 11, 12, 13, feel yourself rising even higher. 14, 15, 16, almost there. 17, 18, 19, number 20, you are there. Take a moment and orient yourself to the superconscious mind level.

Play Ascension Music for 1 Minute

Now from the superconscious mind level you are going to rise up and beyond the karmic cycle and the 5 lower planes to the soul plane. The white light is always with you and you may be assisted by your Masters and Guides as you ascend to the soul plane. Number 1 rising up. 2, 3, 4, rising higher. 5, 6, 7, letting information flow. 8, 9, 10, you are halfway there. 11, 12, 13, feel yourself rising even higher. 14, 15, 16, almost there. 17, 18, 19, number 20, you are there. Take a moment and orient yourself to the soul plane.

Play Ascension Music for 1 Minute

From the soul plane you are able to perceive information from various sources and overview all your past lives, your current lifetime, and future lives, including all your frequencies. Take a few moments now and evaluate this data and choose your next lifetime. Get a feel for the entire process.

Play New Age Music for 6 Minutes

You have done very well. Now I want you to further open up the channels of communication by removing any obstacles and allow yourself to receive information and experiences that will directly apply to and help better your present lifetime. Allow yourself to receive more advanced and more specific information from the higher planes this time. Your Higher Self and Masters and Guides may assist you in receiving this all important information which will help you raise your frequency and improve your karmic subcycle. Do this now.

Play Ascension Music for 8 Minutes

Alright now. Sleep now and rest. You did very well. Listen very carefully. I'm going to count forward now from 1 to 5. When I reach the count of 5 you will be back in the present and on the Earth plane. You will be able to remember everything you experienced. You will feel very relaxed, refreshed, and you will be able to do whatever you have planned for the rest of the day or evening. You will feel very positive about what you've just experienced and very motivated about your confidence and ability to play this tape again to experience the soul plane. Alright now. 1 very, very deep. 2 you're getting a little bit lighter. 3 you're getting much, much lighter. 4 very, very light. 5 awaken wide awake and refreshed.

Finally, you are now prepared for actual ascension. This last exercise is a soul plane ascension, with one main difference. The purification of your soul, the attainment of grace and the complete elimination of all need to reincarnate will now be initiated as you practice this technique:

Ascension/State of Grace

Now listen very carefully. I want you to imagine a bright white light coming down from above and entering the top of your head. Filling your entire body. See it, feel it and it becomes reality. Now imagine an aura of pure white light emanating from your heart region. Again surrounding your entire body. Protecting you. See it, feel it and it becomes reality. Now only your Higher Self, Masters and Guides and highly evolved loving entities who mean you well will be able to influence you during this or any other hypnotic session. You are totally protected by this aura of pure white light.

In a few moments I am going to count from 1 to 20. As I do so you will feel yourself rising up to the superconscious mind level where you will be able to receive information from your Higher Self and your Masters and Guides. Number 1 rising up. 2, 3, 4 rising higher. 5, 6, 7, letting information flow. 8, 9, 10,

you are halfway there. 11, 12, 13, feel yourself rising even higher. 14, 15, 16, almost there. 17, 18, 19, number 20, you are there. Take a moment and orient yourself to the superconscious mind level.

Play Ascension Music for 1 Minute

Now from the superconscious mind level you are going to rise up and beyond the karmic cycle and the five lower planes to the soul plane. The white light is always with you and you may be assisted by your Masters and Guides as you ascend to the soul plane. Number 1 rising up. 2, 3, 4, rising higher. 5, 6, 7, letting information flow. 8, 9, 10, you are halfway there. 11, 12, 13, feel yourself rising even higher. 14, 15, 16, almost there. 17, 18, 19, number 20, you are there. Take a moment and orient yourself to the soul plane. Perceive the sound of a single note of a flute.

Play Ascension Music for 1 Minute

Mentally picture your Higher Self as a human-looking being guiding you through your ascension. Your Higher Self gives you an elixir to drink. This purification drink assists in preparing your soul for perfection. Drink this liquid now. Your Higher Self now reviews your Akashic records with you and points out any remaining karma. Imagine a fire beside you. Place a card with notations of your remaining karma one at a time in this fire. Your soul is being purified as the cards are consumed by the flame. Do this now.

Play Ascension Music for 3 Minutes

Now begin the process of opening up your third eye and activating each of your seven major chakras. Perceive the first chakra turning red and becoming activated and aligned. See the second chakra turn orange, the third yellow, the fourth green, the fifth blue, the sixth indigo and the seven or crown chakra violet. Each of these seven chakras are perfectly aligned and activated.

Now activate the eight chakras on the fourth dimension and

the seven chakras on the fifth dimension. All 22 chakras are aligned and their colors merge into a brilliant white light. Do this now.

Play Ascension Music for 3 Minutes

Now see yourself merging with the white light. Your Higher Self has resumed its form as the white light and you are merging and becoming one with it. You are one with the creator. You are one with the universe. Now you are ready to ascend to the higher planes. You have attained grace. Do this now.

Play Ascension Music for 6 Minutes

Alright now. Sleep now and rest. You did very well. Listen very carefully. I'm going to count forward now from 1 to 5. When I reach the count of 5 you will be back in the present and on the Earth plane. You will be able to remember everything you experienced. You will feel very relaxed, refreshed, and you will be able to do whatever you have planned for the rest of the day or evening. You will feel very positive about what you've just experienced and very motivated about your ability to play this tape again to experience the soul plane and prepare for ascension. Alright now. 1 very, very deep. 2 you're getting a little bit lighter. 3 you're getting much, much lighter. 4 very, very light. 5 awaken wide awake and refreshed.

Since it is necessary to clinically die, or cross into spirit to ascend, we will discuss the concept of death. There is a great difference between the Eastern view of this phenomenon and how we in the West look upon the concept of death.

I will utilize the Tibetan theology, as presented by the *Tibetan Book of the Dead*, to present the Eastern view. The Western perspective will be summarized by the reports of near-death experiences (NDEs) by Westerners, and Christian theology.

One common observation of patients describing near-death experiences is that the consciousness at death was so similar to that of life that they were unable to recognize the fact that they experienced a shift in realities. This is in agreement with the Tibetan belief that all of the bardo states (including life, death, in-between life, rebirth, dreams and meditation) are equivalent. These various states all possess a similar mechanism of continuity in the space-time component of our universe.

The following chart represents components of NDEs as described by Westerners:

Noise Before or While Leaving the Body
Buzzing inside head, ringing, click, roar, banging, whistling, wind, whooshing sound in ears, wind bells in the distance, majestic music.

The Tunnel
Rectangular tunnel, round tunnel turning into square, tube, cylinder, tunnel with concentric circles, impenetrable dark valley, funnel.

The Dark Void
Vacuum, cave, swirling black clouds, black, gray water.

The Nonphysical "Body"
Form: globular version of human body with appendages, without appendages, amorphous cloud, without eyes, no body, pure consciousness, point of consciousness, little ball of energy.

Constitution: mist, wispy, cloud, smoke-like, vapor, transparent, cloud of colors, orange-yellow-blue/indigo, no colors, white, glowing composed of light, energy pattern, charged, weightless, airy like a feather, words can't describe, comfortable warmth.

Senses: heightened vision, hearing, occasionally smell and taste, no touch, no pressure, zoom up and back with vision.

Mobility: can move quickly from place to place, passes through solids, timeless, time speeded up.

Consciousness: can read other's thoughts, no vocabulary

to thoughts picked up, speak to greeters with the mind.

Border or Transition to the Light
Door, fog, rainbow bridge across the sky, beautiful glowing arch.

The Light's Form
Color: white, crystal clear, yellowish white, amber, very bright, surrounded by blackness, its rays do not penetrate the tunnel, sparkles around it.

Constitution: can't see through it.

Form: totally encompassing, rectangular, huge beam, a glowing cloud.

Quality: loving, warm, accepting, kind, safe, joy, comfort, pleasure, euphoric, calming, perfect understanding, complete knowledge, perfect love, overwhelming compassion.

Communication: direct thought transfer, no language, a voice.

The Border Between This World and the Other World
Lake, river, body of water, gray mist, field of flowers, a line, a line intuited but not perceived, a waterfall, edge of the tunnel with a sea of light beyond.[1,2,3]

---

[1] R. Moody, "Life After Life" (New York: Bantam, 1975).

[2] M. Morse, "Closer to the Light" (New York: Villard, 1990).

[3] K. Ring, "Life at death: A scientific investigation of the near-death experience" (New York: Coward, McCann, and Geoghegan, 1980).

The Easterners view death as an opportunity for learning and spiritual growth, as is life. Since the death process involves freewill and choice, it affords possibilities for both the creation of personal experiences and evolvement of the soul.

The lesson of accepting both the positive and negative aspects of our personality and joining them from the point of view of light is well delineated when the journeying soul confronts the Peaceful and Wrathful Buddhas during bardo. The absolute love represented by the Clear Light is its most important paradigm.

It is not enough simply to accept the dark parts of our being, but to psychologically integrate it and overcome the duality of light and darkness through merging with the Wrathful Buddhas. When this is accomplished, they achieve perfection and may ascend to join Buddha.

Emotional detachment characterizes the early phases of death, according to the Easterners. It is only in later phases of bardo that the emotional components resurface. The Chos-nyid and Srid-pa'i Bardos represent fear for many transitees, and can result in a rebirth through emotional attractions to images of their future parents.

Other desires manifest in late phases of death, such as having a family, desires for a body and other forms of co-dependencies. These will result in a rebirth accompanied by a carryover of karmic debts into the new life.

Both Eastern and Western concepts of death depict this state as a disembodied consciousness. A more subtle and immaterial body is perceived only as death progresses. These descriptions are not unlike the nature of ghosts as reported in the occultist and parapsychological literature, as well as cross cultural folklore.

Differences Between Eastern and Western Views of Death

We can note several differences between Christian (NDE) and Tibetan views of the death state and what is observed in-between life. These can be listed as follows:

1.   Christians report encountering angels, Jesus, the Light and other spirit guides. The Tibetans report communication with Buddhas and other deities.

2.   Christians more commonly report a white or golden bright light, whereas the Clear Light is seen by the Easterners.

3.   Tibetans do not report hearing heavenly music, whereas Westerners do.

4.   Mahayana Tibetan scripture stresses the concept of the universe as ultimate one of Mind, rather than Love. It also focuses on the Paths of Meditation and Knowledge as the mechanism for attaining ascension. Christian theology stresses the Path of Love.

5.   Whereas Tibetans present a paradigm of karma and judgment for motivating spiritual growth, Westerners preach forgiveness.

We can see a significant departure of philosophy from these five factors. The Christian Light imparts the message that love is the main lesson to be learned in physical life. Knowledge acquisition is secondary. The NDEs of Tibetans stress the acquisition of knowledge about the self and nature of reality.

Christians are attracted to the Light, which is associated with bliss and ecstatic love. The Tibetans may avoid the Clear

Light, and report fear of the deities they encounter. Westerners report panoramic life reviews that foster their spiritual growth and understanding. The Easterners describe a judgment ending in dismemberment.

The Tibetan is left alone to face challenging tests in bardo. Westerners describe the presence of loving entities, including religious figures and departed loved ones, who support them and impart helpful instructions. Rebirth or the Western soul is more commonly directed by bonds of love to their family. Primal desires, or concepts of the mind, are usually why the Tibetan reincarnates.

When we consider the theology of Roman Catholic beliefs, some interesting differences arise in their NDEs reported. The Catholic theology of the Late Middle Ages depicted death as a form of judgment and evaluation of the soul. Gallup polls have shown that about 60 percent of Americans currently adhere to the concept and belief of hell.[4] This would involve an assessment of the soul.

Christian NDE reports do not reflect this judgment or weighing of the soul. What we find instead is a supportive life review surrounded by loving entities. The Roman Catholic belief from the Late Middle Ages that a battle between good and evil forces over the soul of the departed is also in contrast to Christian NDEs, as I have already described.

Christian survivors of attempted suicide report typical NDEs involving love and life reviews, as well as the experience of compassion emanating from the Light. Theological paradigms would suggest their soul would be

---

[4] J. L. Sheler, "Hell's sober comeback." U.S. News & World Report, 110 (March 25, 1991): 56-64.

doomed to hell for this act.

Children of Westerners report the presence of "angels without wings."[5] Those children brought up in the Eastern philosophies reported NDEs in which they saw God as an old man with a beard. Some Mormon children depicted their NDEs as their soul being taken to Jesus by angelic guardians. These guardians are not a component of Mormon theology. Those data strongly suggest that both the Eastern and Western NDEs reported are not strongly influenced by cultural factors.

We can see a commonality in the concept of oneness depicted in both Eastern and Western views of death. For example, the Tibetan books of the dead emphasize that the outer and inner reality are truly one. All these illusions are produced by the mind, and are merely thought-forms. Christ taught a similar concept of oneness of our inner and outer universe when he stated, "I am my brother's keeper" and "Do unto others as you would have them do unto you."

Death and Time Concepts

Tibetan theology describes a changing nature of time following physical death. Parallels can be drawn between Tibetan views of death and Tantric meditation. After beginning with a sequence of mental imaging, Tantric meditation culminates with the revealing of the Clear Light of the quieted minds. There is no sense of time when this occurs.

This expansion of folding of time is also reported by shamans, allowing the shaman to physically traverse space faster than would otherwise be possible. Geronimo, the

---

[5] M. Morse, op. cit.

famous Apache shaman, supposedly lengthened nights so that he and his tribe would be able to travel great distances and escape capture by the American soldiers.[6]

We can see from this depiction that in-between experiences of time and space are possible. Our perception of these concepts represent a physical plane illusion or maya. The possibilities of expanded time can be delineated as follows:

A uniform, continuous scale time and space of reality.

1. Contracted or expanded continuous-scale time and space.
2. Ordinal-scale space and time composed of sequences and directions with unclear durations and distances.
3. Holographic time devoid of time or space, also described as simultaneous time.

A commonality concerning time, space and the potential for learning, for our consciousness exists in both Tibetan and Western paradigms. Life and death space share certain similarities in meanings and purpose.

We learn based on our choices in-between lives. Opportunities for growth abound, and although specific lessons may vary personally and culturally, there may remain in death more essential human adventures: to accept darkness with light from the point of view of light and to integrate both, and to deepen both our capacity to love and our understanding of reality and the self.

---

[6] A. Debo, "Geronimo: The man, his time, his place" (Norman, OK: University of Oklahoma Press, 1976).

The dark tunnel so often described in Western NDEs has parallels with other theologies. For instance, the dark tunnel is also thought to be the interior of the body in the views of traditional shamanism, contemporary alternative healing, and some contemporary Christian philosophy. A shaman might journey into the dark-tunnel interior of a patient's body to find and diagnose an illness and effect a cure. The alternative healer may view the tunnel experience in NDEs to be the soul going up the body along the primary energy axis of the spine and leaving the body in the bright light of the crown chakra. Some contemporary Christian theology may look upon the tunnel experience as the transition of the soul from inside to outside the body when the soul has remained "in the body longer than is necessary after the body begins to die." It is said to be optional; a more timely and direct release circumvents the tunnel experience.[7]

The Principle of Oneness

The concept of Oneness is proposed by all the major religions of the world. The Judeo-Christian God, the Hindu Brahman, the Sufi Hidden Essence and the Buddhist Dharma-kaya are but a few examples. Each of these paradigms transcends the dualism and separation of our physical plane in space and time.

Various paths are presented by these religions to achieve this oneness. Included among these paths are meditation and contemplation, devotion, service, love and Paths of Knowledge.

---

[7] H. Smith, "The religions of man" (New York: Harper Perennials, 1986).

In Hinduism, these five paths are classified as the four yogas, literally means for yoking or joining with Oneness. They include the Jnana yoga of intellectual discrimination, the Raja yoga of meditation, the Bhakti yoga of heartfelt love and devotion to a deity and/or other humans, and the Karma yoga of work and service in the world.

We have already discussed the fact that whereas Christianity focuses on the path of essential, unconditional love, Buddhism emphasizes the paths of knowledge and meditation. The First Noble Truth of Buddhism is that of suffering or duhkha. The ego's resistance to change, the self-cherishing nature of ego, an unenlightened perception of things within categories and as separate rather than as essentially one, and misdeeds bring on this suffering.

By coming to know the nature of self and reality, we can overcome this suffering. This is accomplished by experiencing the Oneness of the absolute mind in the form of the Clear Light, or Rigpa.

The practice of compassion is how the Buddhists express love. This emphatic identification with the suffering of others\ is accomplished by a shifting of attention away from the self-cherishing, self-grasping, divisive nature of the ego to the greater whole. The practice of extending lovingkindness to others, i.e., the path of love, is one means for developing compassion.

Compassion requires a mental shift in understanding and perception, which can be achieved through reframing practices such as mirroring and empathy, and which requires meditation.

Oneness is experienced only when the absolute mind is

unveiled through meditation. The mind's illusions are disengaged through meditation, and the compassion component is freed to express itself.

In contrast to Tibetan Buddhism's emphasis on meditation, Christianity emphasizes essential, unconditional love, or what early Christians called agape, as the path to Oneness. Love received from God and extended toward all neighbors regardless of their qualities is the primary vehicle for altering one's perception of reality and overcoming separation.

The difference between Tibetan Buddhism and essential Christianity in their emphasis on paths toward Oneness is directly reflected in their broadest views of the nature of reality. In Buddhism, ultimately the one true reality is Mind, the formless unconditioned Truth and Light of Dharma-kaya. In a contrasting focus in Christianity, God's "infinite Love" is central. The universe is basically friendly and safe in that God provides all people their needs through His love, which is the source from which a Christian can love and help all others unconditionally.

Forgiveness Differences Between

Eastern and Western Concepts

The concept of forgiveness is important when we consider the different paths to ascension. Buddhism differs from essential and contemporary Christianity in its concern about karma. Karma literally means action. The law of karma says in part that the quality of one's future in this life and other lives, including the nature of one's moral being, depends to a great extent on one's current actions. Thus, karma conceptually links the quality of a person's nature—one's moral character —to the person's actions. By extension, the concept allows the judgment of people by their deeds.

In the Bardol Thödol, the Lord of Death links karma to guilt and fear when it shows the soul its good and bad deeds in the Mirror of Karma.

Christianity emphasizes the use of forgiveness as a vehicle for manifesting unconditional love to others, regardless of their actions. This includes God's forgiveness of all humans, who have already been saved through the Christ. Thus, the person is conceptually separated from his or her deeds and can be loved and accepted unconditionally rather than judged. We can see a vast difference between Buddhism and Christianity in their focus on depictions of the ultimate nature of the universe as Mind or Love, in the paths to Oneness on which they focus, in the relationship of people's nature to their actions, and in the roles of judgment and forgiveness in the dynamics of the cosmos.

Similarities in the two representative experiences include: (1) hearing loud noises such as a wind or roar early in the death process; (2) seeing religious figures like Buddhas or Jesus; (3) seeing a white or gold Light that is separate from oneself, defining a dualistic state of consciousness; (4) merging with a brilliant Light to create a sense of Oneness or Dharma-kaya; (5) a life review/judgment; and more generally, (6) events that reveal near-death and death to be learning processes.

The Mechanism of Death

We have discussed the experiences of previews of death

from the Western perspective of NDEs and the Tibetan depiction of death experiences in *The Tibetan Book of the Dead*. Here I will present data from the over 14,000 patients I have worked with since 1974, and whom I have guided to and beyond the death experience.

Death is merely a transition from one dimension to another. It is not a state of termination, for our soul is eternal. The moment of death is characterized by our soul leaving the physical body without experiencing any of the pain or discomfort that others on the physical plane may observe in our former biological shell.

You are now in a position to overview your former body while in your less material astral body. Spirit guides and departed relatives may be present, as your communication with them is entirely by telepathy. Your sense of hearing is extraordinary at this time, and you are able to hear conversations originating from the physical plane. Advance levels of psychic gifts (telepathy, precognition, etc.) are also evident.

The White Light is near you, and represents the only way you can relocate to the soul plane. The silver cord occasionally reported by NDEs is now severed so that your astral body is completely free of its physical counterpart.

If your soul does not enter the White Light you will remain on the astral plane in a disoriented state. The other phenomena noted by NDEs are accurate and will be felt. These include the death sounds, tunnel and so on.

Eventually, your soul enters the White Light, which represents your higher self, and you are transported to the soul plane. It is here that your higher self and Masters and Guides will advise you in your selection of a future life. If you have successfully applied the techniques presented in this book, ascension will be an option. The other possibility is to remain as a guide to other evolving souls.

Death is a state of expanding beyond oneself. The White Light's brilliance supersedes all awareness during the initial phase of this process. This death space is a nonphysical world of total freedom and pure consciousness.

The bliss represented by death is due to a oneness with our higher self and a removal of the mind-created illusions. We are finally free.

In summary, we can list the characteristics of the death state as follows:

1.   A brilliant White Light is seen.
2.   There is no pain.
3.   Peace and love are noted immediately.
4.   The soul emerges and is transformed to be with its higher and perfect self.
5.   The silver cord is severed.
6.   Telepathy and other ESP are exhibited.
7.   Unusual sounds are heard.
8.   The tunnel experience begins.
9.   The presence of other loving entities is felt.
10.   There is total awareness of the physical world left behind and the nonphysical one just entered.

The purpose of ascension techniques is to utilize this death process to place our soul in a state of perfection so that we can finally rid ourselves of the necessity of future lives within a karmic cycle.

We must not ignore the potential for healing afforded by

death. The death state provides our soul with the opportunity for growing, learning and healing through the application of love, knowledge-based understanding and the integration of opposites present in this transitory state of consciousness we call death. Do not fear this state, as it is a necessary condition that we must face many times in order to finally ascend and rid ourselves for the necessity of this experience.

The goal of *The Tibetan Book of the Dead* is to show the voyaging soul that the mind creates many illusions concerning the death experience that result in unnecessary fear.

Eliminating this fear and merging with the higher self represented by the Clear Light is the only way to achieve nirvana and ascend.

Spiritual empowerment will always be manifested when we eliminate fear and forgo the separation of our conscious-ness into ego, with the resulting fear of losing this ego state. When we no longer identify our essence with the physical, emotional or mental transitory form of our being, we are ready for ascension.

Chapter 15

The Attainment of Grace

_____

W e discussed the state of grace in Chapter 1. Here the culmination of the various approaches presented in this book will be tied in to the concept of ascension. The first obstacle in our goal of attaining grace is our consciousness.

Our normal state of awareness is distorted, clouded and mostly out of control. The Bhagavad Gita stated this observation over 2,000 years ago:

> "Restless (the) mind is,
> So strongly shaken
> In the grip of the senses;
> Gross and grown hard
> With stubborn desire. . . . .
> Truly, I think
> The wind is no wilder."[1]

This realization that we are distracted from our path back to God is the first step in making ascension a viable reality. Even though our subconscious is clouded, we still have the potential to realign our soul's energy and place ourselves on the

_____

[1] S. Prabhavanda and C. Isherwood, "The Bhagavad Gita" (New York): New American Library, 1944).

path to grace.

Plato averred: "In order that the mind should see the light instead of darkness, so the entire soul must be turned away from this changing world, until its eye can bear to contemplate reality and that supreme splendor which we call the God. Hence there may well be an art whose aim would be to affect this very thing."[2]

In order to attain the state of grace and place ourselves in the position to be able to ascend, we must master six disciplines. These can be listed as follows:

1.   Emotional transformation
2.   Redirection of awareness
3.   Refinement of awareness
4.   Concentration
5.   Ethical training
6.   The development of wisdom

Emotional Transformation

In establishing an emotional transformation we must first reduce and then eliminate destructive emotions such as anger and fear. This clear awareness and cleansing of these emotional responses is a prerequisite to the second phase of this transformation.

The cultivation of positive emotions such as compassion, joy and love has been described already in Chapter 7. This is the second phase of emotional transformation. Christians speak of agape, and Buddhist's compassion is represented by

---

[2] Plato, "The Republic." Trans. F. Cornford (Oxford: Oxford University Press, 1945).

Bhakti's love.   These can be achieved only through an unconditional love and acceptance that applies to all people and things without exception.

The third component of emotional transformation is the cultivation of equanimity.   When we establish a mental equilibrium, the ability to love and express compassion as unconditional responses, even during times of stress, becomes a part of our psyche. This concept has been expressed before as the Christian Father's "divine apatheia," the Buddhist's equanimity, the Hindu's samatva which leads to a "vision of sameness," and the Taoist principle of "the equality of things," which leads beyond "the trouble of preferring one thing to another."

Redirection of Awareness

We can apply yogic techniques, including meditation, and self-hypnosis to accomplish a redirection of our awareness. The exercises I have presented will train you to accomplish this goal.

When we place more emphasis on giving than receiving, our desires that divert us from the path toward grace become less self-centered.   Accompanying this is a shift in our motivation, which is now more focused as we move from egocentric (self-centered)to allocentric (concern for others) levels.

This shift represents a cleansing of our soul and a detachment from the material world. We also experience a reduction in compulsive behavior and a serene disenchantment with the things of the world which no longer exert a blinding fascination or compulsive pull. This is the Buddhist nibbidda and the yogic viraga and is the basis of the Athenian philosopher Epicurus's claim that the way to make people happy is not to add to their riches but to reduce their desires. Buddha stated this principle in his Third Noble Truth when he proposed the idea that the end of craving leads to the end of suffering.

As we reduce these compulsive cravings, our intrapsychic conflicts correspondingly decrease. This is an important goal, but not easy to obtain without undergoing some form of training. Practicing the exercises presented in this book will make your task all the more attainable with less discouraging results.

Refinement of Awareness

Since our usual state of mind represents an awareness that is both impaired and insensitive, we must refine it. Most of us exhibit scattered desires, emotional instability and poor attention spans. These characteristics function to further divert us from our attainment of grace.

Our goal in this stage is to render our perception to be more sensitive, more accurate, and more appreciative of the freshness and novelty of each moment of experience. Intuitive capacities, usually blunted or blinded, are to be cultivated. The self-hypnosis and meditation techniques I have selected for your training are designed to increase the sensitivity of both your internal and external perception so that colors seem brighter, and the inner world becomes more available.

One of the many advantages of refinement of outer perception is an accompanying refinement of inner intuitive capacities. This introspective sensitization was presented when the ancient wisdom traditions speak of the development of an inner perceptual organ or the opening of an inner eye: the eye of the soul (Plato), the eye of the heart (Sufism), the eye of the Tao (Taoism), the third eye (Tibetan), or the Western philosophers' nous or intellectus.

By training our mind to maintain our focus on the present, the result is a present-centered freshness of perception variously described as mindfulness (Buddhism), anuragga (Hinduism), the "sacrament of the present moment" (Christianity), the "draught of forgetfulness" in which one forgets the past and comes anew into each present moment (Steiner), and characteristic of self-actualizers (Maslow). Awareness by itself can be seen to be quite curative. When it is combined with ascension techniques it fosters our ability to attain the state of grace.

Concentration

The development of concentration is of paramount importance in attaining any goal. It increases in significance when spiritual quests are sought. Being able to direct attention at will is so important because the mind tends to take on qualities of the objects to which it attends. For example, thinking of an angry person tends to elicit anger while thinking of a loving person may elicit feelings of love. The person who can control concentration can therefore control and cultivate specific emotions and motive.

Western psychology has expressed more than a cynical attitude toward establishing focused concentration. William James, the father of American psychology, concluded that "Attention cannot be continuously sustained. . . . The faculty of voluntarily bringing back a wandering attention over and over again is the very root of judgement, character and will. No one is compos sui if he have it not. An education which would improve this faculty would be the education par excellence. It is easier to define this ideal than to give practical direction for bringing it about."[3]

If we are to rise above Western psychological brain-washing, we must observe this contrast between traditional Western psychology, which says attention cannot be sustained, and the art of ascension, which says that attention can and must be sustained.

Ethical Training

Ethics is an essential discipline both for the mind and the fate of our soul. Unethical behavior both stems from and reinforces destructive mental factors such as greed and anger. Conversely, ethical behavior undermines these and cultivates mental factors such as kindness, compassion and calm. As a result of spiritual growth through exercises herein given, we can direct our ethical behavior to flow spontaneously as a natural expression of identification with all people and all life.

The Development of Wisdom

There is quite a difference between knowledge and wisdom. Knowledge is simply the possession of certain facts or data. To exhibit wisdom is to apply this knowledge in a manner that benefits others, or our own spiritual growth. Something we must be is an apt description of this element

---

[3] W. James, "Talks to teachers on psychology and to students on some of life's ideals" (New York: Dover, 1962).

necessary to reach the state of grace.

With a deeply developed wisdom we come to understand that all suffering ends when we transform our self by raising our consciousness to the point of perfection. The wisdom component of this paradigm is far beyond mere concepts, images or thoughts. It concerns itself with the nature of our consciousness, and its relationship to God and the universe.

A special form of insight is developed as we acquire this liberating wisdom. Since liberation is our goal in attaining grace and ascension, this wisdom is critical to our spiritual evolution. Other terms that have been applied to this element are in the East jnana (Hinduism), prajna (Buddhism), or ma'rifah (Islam), and in the West as gnosis or scientia sacra.

These six components to attaining the state of grace are highly interdependent and the development of one fosters the development of others. Some traditions focus more on some processes than on others. For example, Indian philosophy divides practices into various yogas. All of them acknowledge ethics as an essential foundation. Raja yoga emphasizes meditation and the training of attention and awareness; Bhakti yoga is more emotional and focuses on the cultivation of love; Karma yoga uses work in the world to refine motivation, and Jnana yoga hones the intellect and wisdom.

An Eastern Example of the Attainment of Grace

Westerners are quite familiar with the resurrection of Jesus as an example of ascension. The story of Buddah's attainment of Grace is not so well known, so I summarize it here.

Siddhattha Gutama, or the Buddha, joined a group of ascetics in the search of spiritual truth. He engaged in such a rigorous discipline of denial of the body's biological needs that he nearly died of starvation.

Frustrated by his attempts he left this group and came to a peaceful place on a tributary by the Ganges River. He sat beneath a bo-tree and committed himself to a meditation that would not be terminated until he attained enlightenment.

The Evil One, Mara, and his three daughters tried everything in their power to tempt and dissuade Buddha from his quest. Gutama's dedication won out in the end and he became the enlightened Buddha we know of today. He entered a transcendental and eternal realm of being.

For an additional week Buddha remained in meditation and then explored the local village. There he again met Mara, who urged him to depart the physical plane and enter nirvana. The Buddha declined this ascension offer and declared that he must first proclaim the Dhamma to others. Buddha decided to remain as a guide until the last mortal attained grace.

A Western Example of the Attainment of Grace

Annalee Skarin was an author and devout Mormon, who lived with a Mrs. B. in her home in Salt Lake City, Utah. Annalee informed Mrs. B. on June 16, 1952 that she (Annalee) was about to undergo ascension or translation.

Mrs. B. awoke suddenly at 1:10 A.M. on June 17 to the strong aroma that appeared to fill the entire house. When she entered Annalee's room, all she found was Mrs. Skarin's dentures on a bedside table and all of Annalee's clothes in her closet.

That evening at around 10:30 P.M., Mrs. B and her son and two daughters witnessed Annalee entering the living room wearing a plain blue dress. Annalee asked them, "Do you believe I have translated?" When Mrs. B and her children acknowledged this feat, Annalee invoked blessings upon them.

At that moment Mrs. Skarin transformed herself into a shining being in white raiment, with her hair surrounded by a golden light. Annalee smiled showing her new and gleaming teeth, even though the only set of dentures she had remained on the bedside table. Following further prayer and blessings, Annalee disappeared slowly from sight.

Over the years there have been reports of sightings of Annalee Skarin. For example, in October of 1952 nearly 100 people acknowledged attending a talk given by Annalee Skarin and her late husband, Reason Skarin, at the New Age Press Book Center in Los Angeles.

Mormon church officials reported finding her in Los Angeles in 1956. In 1963 she contacted her publishers through a female agent! Annalee Skarin taught her readers that death was unnecessary and that we can overcome and avoid death.

The mysterious circumstances concerning Annalee Skarin's disappearances and reappearances propagated rumors that the Federal Bureau of Investigation (FBI) looked into this matter. It is purported that the FBI was forced to terminate its investigation due to lack of concrete evidence of foul play.

The Ultimate Experience of Grace

We have seen throughout this book that there is great difficulty in the path back to God. If this were not accurate, then anyone, no matter how evil, could return to God in a matter of moments.

To attain grace and reach God by ascension we must live

dangerously. By this I mean that we must move far beyond the material world and involve ourselves with spiritualism and psychic empowerment. This undoubtedly will bring criticism from those in our social circle and sphere of influence.

To attain grace is to witness the ineffable experience of being within the brilliant Light of the higher planes. The human mind cannot adequately relate to this phenomena. Only experience and spiritual evolution can bring this beauty and love to our very essence. We are ourselves a part of this infinite awareness of God.

Here are two stories concerning the quest for enlightenment. Both of these tales originate from India, where it is the custom to develop spiritually under the direction of a guru. In this first tale a young man asked a great spiritual teacher to teach him to ascend. The guru said that he would grant the student's request, but only for a sizable amount of gold.

As the student had no money, he asked the wise teacher what to do. The guru instructed him to go out and acquire it. Many years later the student approached the guru and presented him with the requisite amount of gold he had earned.

The wise man returned the gold to the student and informed him that he did not need this gold, for he held the gold of God within his soul. The guru went further in his declaration and informed the student that he would now teach him all he knew, free.

When the student asked the guru why he required the gold fee in the first place, the sage responded by stating that if he hadn't learned anything from life during the process of acquiring this gold, he couldn't teach him anything. Since he had fulfilled this goal, he was ready to learn.

The moral of this tale is that the experience of life is necessary to transform our knowledge into wisdom. We must accept this concept and make it a part of our consciousness.

During the early days of Indian history a group of pilgrims traveled to visit a great saint. One student of a local guru, who was impatient with his process in spiritual growth, decided to leave his teacher and join the pilgrimage to visit the great saint.

Several months later this disgruntled student returned to his teacher and admitted that he was wrong to leave his guru, for the only holy grounds in the area were those by the guru.

The rishi's reply shocked the student. This wise old sage informed the young man that since God is everywhere, all grounds are sacred and holy. Your realization of His presence is within you. This is why we must look within ourselves to attain grace and finally ascend.

Once we attain the ultimate experience of grace it becomes a part of us, and we in turn become a part of the divine nature of God. This ultimate experience requires us to enter the realm of the higher planes to view the universe the way it truly works, free of illusions. The fastest route to this goal is by accessing the remnant of God energy within us known as our higher self.

God-realization

We can trace man's interest in attaining grace back to the earliest religions. These were the Mystery Schools. They taught their initiates techniques to reawaken their latent intuitive powers and prepared them to receive enlightenment.

Hypnosis was part of this training and utilized to heighten consciousness with the goal of experiencing a oneness with

Ultimate Reality. Many of its graduates claimed a direct and intuitive access to spiritual wisdom.

The belief that God is at the core of all reality and we are all One, a part of the divine spark of God's energy, was the belief this system was based on. These Mystery Schools spread throughout antiquity, and we find traces of this goal of attaining grace by mystery rites in such ancient cultures as:

8.   The Vedic religion of India.
9.   Orphic and Bacchic rites in Greece.
10. Chinese Taoism.
11. Egyptian cults.
12. The Mithraic and Magian schools of central Asia.
13. The Mayas of Central America.
14. The Native American religions of North America.

Some of these teachings carried over into Jewish and Christian traditions. The early Jewish mystics, for instance, used meditation to encounter a symbolic chariot that carried them to meet God.

Freemasons began to appear in twelfth-century medieval Europe, and brought with them the magnificent Gothic cathedrals (most likely inspired by the buildings characteristic of the astral plane), in addition to ancient spiritual truths descended from the Mystery Schools.

The Masonic lore refers to their grand architecture as a metaphor for the process by which a Mason became a "regenerated perfected man" with larger consciousness and faculties, an efficient instrument for use by the Great Architectin His plan of rebuilding the Temple of fallen humanity"[4]

The Mystery Schools were persecuted by the other religions because of their insistence that anyone could experience Ultimate Truth directly—without the need of a religious or political agent.

Although the doctrines of these ancient schools were prohibited, they appeared in the popular culture carefully disguised. One example is the mystery plays of the Middle Ages, during which the performers danced out the Mystery School paradigm using various codes. Some of these messages were hidden in the songs sung by the troubadours so that only initiates could decipher their true meaning.

Hall summarized the true purpose of these mysteries when he wrote, "The real purpose of modern Masonry is the expediting of the spiritual evolution of those who aspire to perfect their own nature and transform it into a more godlike quality."[5]

We see that all throughout history humankind has made desperate attempts to find a solution to the problem of ascension. The artificiality and co-dependency exhibited by religions and political structures, since the first state was established in ancient Egypt, has failed miserably to fulfill this goal of God-Realization.

Throughout the more than 35,000 past-life regressions and future-life progressions I have conducted since 1974, I can personally testify to the fact that we all have been here hundreds if not thousands of times before. The system has

---

[4] M. P. Hall, "The Adepts in the Western Tradition" (Los Angeles: Philosophical Research Society, 1951).
[5] M. P. Hall, op. cit.

failed, or we have not gotten it, since our karmic cycle is alive and strong.

We can summarize the problems of our human condition with five words: despair, dread, anxiety, loneliness and death. Until we raise our soul's energy and rise above these dysfunctional vulnerabilities, we are stuck in the karmic cycle.

Society tends to offer us little in the form of true spiritual development. Western thought especially focuses on sharpening our intellect, and incorrectly assumes that knowledge is the criteria that will ensure the attainment of God-Realization. This is an illusion, for knowledge alone will only make us well-educated neurotics, chained to the karmic cycle and miserable at best.

The answer to God-Realization is not complicated. It requires us to look within, not without, for our salvation and eternal bliss. As you progress along your path to ascension, you will learn things that you could not possibly comprehend or appreciate in your human state trapped within the physical body.

This is why I emphasize out-of-body experiences so much in Chapter 13. Only on leaving the confines of our physical shell and merging with our higher self can we truly be one with God.

By conscientiously practicing the exercises in this book you will enter a path that will eventually introduce you to God. This God-Realization is characterized by functioning as a co-word with the One. You will have the privilege of residing in eternal peace and happiness. The ultimate awareness of God is within your grasp. To attain this state of grace and ascend to God you must always look within yourself and learn the technique of merging with your higher self.

We must never forget one of the main themes of this book. It is not necessary to die to attain grace. Most religions incorrectly tell us that we must wait until after the death of the physical body to attain the spiritual freedom we desire.

The purpose of these exercises I have carefully selected is to make this training easier and more efficient. Those of you who decide to use the tapes I recommended in Chapter 13 will find this system even more compatible with a busy lifestyle.

Metaphysical or theological speculation alone will not result in God-Realization. No feeling, mental device, logic, rationalization or any such needy physical plane directive is going to direct you to the path to God. You must earn this glory, and the exercises herein included will facilitate your quest for eternal bliss.

My purpose in writing this book is not to condemn or ridicule religions. My Los Angeles office receives many referrals from ministers, priests, rabbis and even gurus. Most of these individuals mean well.

However, we must take a realistic look at the various religions around today. The sexual scandals of the Catholic Church make international headlines. The tendency for these religions to frighten the public by saying that if you don't believe in Jesus or Buddha, or whomever, you are destined to spend eternity in hell is quite beyond my tolerance.

This petty and insecure stance by the clergy shows their own lack of God-Realization. I have studied the Old Testament, New Testament and Koran in detail. From my perspective, the modern-day versions of these well-meaning religions don't even come close to accurately representing what is in their scriptures. The Old Testament and New Testament have been edited over 18 times during the past 1,800 years!

Life is difficult on the Earth plane and throughout the karmic cycle. Each of us must seek our own path to God. It is not politically correct to ignore the unrest of the world and look within ourselves for enlightenment. This is what we must do, however. We have to ignore all the distractions, temptations and rationalizations contained in this illusory plane and move on to the higher plane. This can only be attained from within our own consciousness.

*O*ur universe is the result of God's plan. Because we possess a divine spark within us known as the Higher Self, we create our own microcosm of this universe. The defense mechanisms, or ego, part of our personality are subjected to the illusions of the material world.

Some of the energy patterns that formed our universe are beyond our control. The yearly revolution of the Earth around the sun and our own solar system's stately progress through space are the products of minds far greater than ours and therefore not subject to our influence. But we are the makers of our own destiny. Part of this destiny is to perfect our soul and ascend to God.

Each of us designs a blueprint for our spiritual evolution before our soul enters the physical body to begin the sojourn on the Earth plane we call life. This framework is subject to change, to improve or lower the ability to enter the path to God at the conclusion of this physical incarnation.

The deepest realities of our spiritual life are often those that we examine the last. We are not aware of the way in which they make us open to the infinite nature of God. God and the soul are two mysterious realities, but their union is equally a mystery that only the Spirit of God, the bond between them, can reveal to the eyes of the heart.

William James, the father of American psychology, stated it most succinctly when he averred, "Most people live, whether physically, intellectually or morally, in a very restricted circle of their potential being. They make use of a very small portion of their possible consciousness. . . . We all have reservoirs of life to draw upon, of which we do not dream.."[1]

Our spiritual destiny is to return to God. This ascension represents the end of our karmic cycle. Everything that receives its being from Him is created to return to Him. God therefore gives each of us the potential to reach its end. Because we are both existing as flesh and spirit, our fate can move us upward or downward, either facilitating or retarding, respectively, this spiritual goal. When we are open to receive God's grace our soul rises up like a flame to rejoin God, from whence we came.

It is the presence of the divine spark within us, called the superconscious or Higher Self, that makes this ascension possible. All we have to do is turn our intention inward and communicate with this perfect energy component of our soul.

Because of the presence of our Higher Self, we can be even more receptive to the concept that God is everywhere. He is in us as represented by this perfect energy known as the Higher Self.

God is in us too in the presence that we call the state of grace. Because of this presence, we finite beings are able to experience Him in this world and to recover the purity of our original image. He is at the end when grace, which is at the beginning of glory, has been fully and definitely opened up and

---

[1] W. James, "Principles of Psychology" (New York: Doubleday, 1950).

we see Him as He is and are like Him and totally deified and function as coworkers in the higher planes.

The greatest glory that we can give Him is to consent to his eternal intention to love us and to be fully aware of His presence in us and in the whole of the universe. He is the only one in whom we can trust, and His faithfulness is as perfect as His truth and the reality of his presence. Accessing our Higher Self places us in direct contact with the God energy. As we practice the exercises presented in this book and raise our level of consciousness, the more completely we remove all obstacles on the path back to Him. As this is accomplished, the more fully our soul will respond to the call of that grace which invites all of us—and has always invited us—to be gods by sharing God's divinity.

This is a perfect time for ascension. On February 3, 1962, a rare event occurred in the constellation Aquarius, the first alignment of seven planets in 80 years. This was the beginning of the Age of Aquarius. A "Harmonic Convergence" took place on August 16 and August 17,1987. This alignment of six planets further ushered in the New Age. On January 11, 1994 seven planets, along with the sun and moon, aligned in Capricorn. Finally, on January 23, 1997 a rare planetary alignment expressed itself as a perfect six-pointed star.

Jupiter, Uranus and Neptune conjoined together for the first time in nearly 200 years. It was during the Renaissance that we last saw the alignment of the five outermost planets. To many astrologers this truly represents the "dawning of the Age of Aquarius . . . the time of mind's true liberation."

Living in an age of rapid scientific and technical progress, increasing productivity and growing emphasis on personal ambition and stress, we are in urgent need of a powerful counterbalance if we are to be able to return to God by ascension. The human spirit is even vaster than the Earth and more unfathomable than the oceans, and these inner heights and depths are merged with those of the God who lives in us by way of our Higher Self. It is only in the light of the divine and universal presence of the One who is Light itself that we can venture to search in the true homeland of His soul where we will one day reach His end and will never leave again.

God is not present passively or statically. He is a living, active and dynamic presence. He is eternal. It is because He transcends us that nothing can escape His immanence, and in us He is more ourselves than we are. The very fact that God's energy is in us and we are in Him makes ascension possible. It is enough for God to desire for each of us to be raised up to Him and for the immeasurable gap that separates what is created from what is uncreated, what is finite from what is infinite. We, in response to God's plan and infinite goodness, are therefore able to reach the heavens above.

We appeared as the last of God's creatures in this world of bodies and spirits in which the heavenly hierarchies were already present, glorious and bathed in supernatural light. We are both a microcosm, a little world in the great world, because we sum up in ourselves all the realms of creation, and a macrocosm, a great world in a little world, because we transcend, by virtue of our immortal soul, the rest of creation, which was to be the framework within which we complete our destiny.

Because of our immortal soul, we are not only a reflection of God, but also an image of the Creator who, in His unfathomable mystery, has created the essence of His thought and inspired it with the one Spirit of love. This Higher-Self component of our very being is accessible any moment we are ready to communicate with it. On discovering it, we discover also the power to create for ourselves the path back to God and the experience of eternal bliss.

In order to enter the path back to God, we must first heal our soul. This is not as difficult as it may initially appear. As I stated in my book, Soul Healing:

"The first condition necessary for successful soul healing to occur is that one must desire it. Specifically, one may desire more energy, more enjoyment, more fulfillment, or more happiness in one's life. Negative desires include the avoidance of disease, of death, fear of loss, or fear of the unknown. Fear can, however, become a useful stage of soul healing, particularly the fear that occurs when one realizes that one's life is not moving in the desired direction, or that something in one's life is missing. Fear is far more widespread than is generally acknowledged. Most of the time we succeed in ignoring fear or distracting ourselves.

A strong desire for soul healing, no matter how it is felt, is more hopeful to facilitate such healing. After all, desires keep us alive and create our lives.

Stress is only a resistance created by our defense mechanisms, by our need to control, justify, or even understand an event. Learning not to judge events and situations is a great and noble part of soul healing.

At the deepest level, I believe soul healing is inevitable. For some people, the time is now. For others, it may take many years or lifetimes. We have the God-given right to suffer and be miserable for as long as we wish. We can accelerate the process if we desire it. We can ask that the veils be lifted, the clouds depart, and that all the barriers to loving oneself be overcome.

Soul healing can be impeded by an unwillingness to face oneself, or by experiencing a temporary respite from an illness or other negative situation. Illness or misfortune may actually be a way to avoid responsibility, to command the family's attention, to indulge in self-pity and feel sorry for oneself, or to avoid work.

Responsibility involves discipline. Interestingly, the word discipline is derived from the same root as the word disciple. Discipline is an aspect of mastery of the challenge of life. Discipline is not so much a harsh striving to achieve a goal as it is the honing of one's skills in a given area.

Soul healing often involves the exercise of discipline, including the discipline (and courage) to follow one's own guidance. Outside forces (defense mechanisms) which control the body and emotions need to be brought under conscious control. Regimens designed to retrain the body and brain may have to be pursued. One may indeed choose illness to learn discipline. Discipline can be as simple as following a healthy diet and exercising regularly, or it may involve years of working through emotional traumas, tracing the threads of intuition to their sources deep within the psyche. At its most efficient, discipline involves accessing the superconscious mind to heal oneself.

Some people understand the power of faith and prayer. True faith helps one to stop worrying, casting out fear and causing anger about one's condition to evaporate. The exercise of faith removes stress from the body and enhances or allows soul healing to proceed more rapidly.

Openness and willingness to surrender to positive forces are important spiritual aspects of healing. The surrender is not to the illness, but to one's Higher Self or God's will. One must realize that God's will is more powerful than our puny egos. First, one may have to exhaust one's own solutions to eventually arrive at a place of utter despair! This is okay, if this is what it takes, for one to be finally receptive to soul healing.

The good news is that we eventually surrender not only our bad habits, but also our fears, despair, and feelings of smallness and insignificance. All such negativity is eventually placed on the altar of sacrifice and ultimately renounced. Perhaps this is the ultimate goal of healing. We renounce all that is not of God or the Higher Self, and then are truly made over in His image. To be your own soul healer is both your true purpose in the universe, the goal of life, and the aim of this book. This, by definition, will fully empower you."[2]

The road to ascension is the path back to God. As we sometimes fail to see the forest for the trees, the route to liberation is there and clear for those who would use it. The power of the ancients lies deep within you. The key now lies in your hands. I have provided you with all the necessary tools to achieve ascension. Use them wisely and enjoy your life as you desire. Believe in yourself and then all things are possible. Although heaven has always been there for our return, time is of the essence. Do not procrastinate your spiritual unfoldment, as heaven can't wait to welcome you back.

---

[2] B. Goldberg, "Soul Healing," op cit., pp. 255-256.

Bibliography

Budge, E.A.W. *The Book of the Dead.* London: Longman's & Co., 1895.

Cerminara, G. *Many Mansions.* New York: Signet, 1967.

I Cor. 12:7-11.

Debo, A. "Geronimo: The man, his time, his place". Norman, OK: University of Oklahoma Press, 1976.

Eliade, M. "Yoga, Immortality and Freedom." Princeton, N.J.: Princeton University Press, 1970.

Evans-Wenz, W.Y. *The Tibetan Book of the Dead.* New York: Oxford University Press, 1960.

Fortune, D. *The Mystical Qabalah.* York Beach, Maine: Samuel Weiser, 1984.

Goldberg, B. *Soul Healing.* St. Paul: Llewellyn, Pub., 1996.

_____. *Past Lives-Future Lives.* New York: Ballantine, 1988.

_____. *Peaceful Transition: The Art of Conscious Dying and the Liberation of the Soul.* St. Paul: Llewellyn Pub., 1997.

_____. *Look Younger, Live Longer: Add 25 to 50 Years to Your Life, Naturally.* St. Paul: Llewellyn Pub., 1998.

_____. *New Age Hypnosis.* St. Paul: Llewellyn Pub., 1998.

_____. *Protected by the Light: The Complete Book of Psychic Self-Defense.* Tucson, Az: Hats Off Books, 2000.

_____ *Astral Voyages: Mastering the Art of Soul Travel.* St. Paul: Llewellyn Pub., 1999.

Gregory the Great, Pope. "Dialogues" (quoted in Jacques LeGoff, *The Birth of Purgatory,* trans. Arthur Goldhammer [Chicago: University of Chicago Press, 1984]).

Hall, M. P. "The Adepts in the Western Tradition". Los Angeles: Philosophical Research Society, 1951.

Hamlet, 3.1.65-68.

Hugo, V. *Toilers of the Sea.* Trans. Isabel F. Hapgood. Milpitas, CA: Atlantean Press, 1993.

James, W. "Talks to teachers on psychology and to students on some of life's ideals." New York: Dover, 1962.

_____. *Principles of Psychology.* New York: Doubleday, 1950.

John 20:28.

John 1:1-4.

Lati, R. and Hopkins, J. *Death, Intermediate State, and Rebirth in Tibetan Buddhism.* Ithaca, N.Y.: Snow Lion, 1985.

Mark 8:29.

Matt. 24:13.

Moody, R. *Life After Life.* New York: Bantam, 1975.

Morse, M. *Closer to the Light.* New York: Villard, 1990.

Pius XII, Pope. Humani generis in Dondrume, Albert "Foi chretienne et oensee contemporaine: les problems philosophiques souleves dans l'encylique Humani generius," 2nd edition. Louvain: Publications universitaires de Louvain, 1952.

Plato. "The Republic." Trans. F. Cornford. Oxford: Oxford University Press, 1945.

Plotinus. *Enneads.* Trans. Kenneth Guthrie. London: George Bell and Sons, 1918.

_____. *The Essential Plotinus.* Trans. E. O'Brien. Indianapolis: Hackett, 1964.

Prabhavanda, S. and Isherwood, C. *The Bhagavad Gita.* New York: New American Library, 1944.

Ring, K. *Life at death.* New York: Coward, McCann and Geoghegan, 1980.

Russell, G. *The Candle of Vision.* Dorset: Prism Press, 1990.

Sheler, J. L. "Hell's sober comeback.." " U.S. News & World Report," March 25, 1991, 110, 56-64.

Smith, H. "The Religions of Man." New York: Harper Perennials, 1986.

Spencer, S. *Mysticism in World Religion.* New York: Penguin, 1963.

Trismegistus, Hermes. "Corpus Hermeticum." Trans. A. J. Festugière and A. D. Nock. Paris: Societe Edition Les Pelles Lettres, 1945-1954.

Wilbur, K. "The Atman Project." Wheaton, IL: Theosophical Pub., 1980.